D1206517

SUBURBAN
BIGAMY

SUBURBAN
BIGAMY

SIX MILES BETWEEN TRUTH AND DECEIT

MICHAEL S. ZIMMERMAN

CONVERSATION
PUBLISHING

Published by Conversation Publishing.
www.conversationpublishing.com

Printed in the United States of America.
First hardcover edition January 2023.

Cover and layout design by G Sharp Design, LLC.
www.gsharpmajor.com

Hardcover ISBN: 979-8-9852879-6-7
Ebook ISBN: 979-8-9852879-7-4

This book is a memoir. It reflects the author's present recollections of past experiences over time. Some names and identifying characteristics of real individuals have been changed to protect their privacy interests.

"I was just a man who couldn't say no."

NORMAN ZIMMERMAN

CONTENTS

INTRODUCTION

"*Get out of my fucking house!*" she screamed at me. Turning her rage to my father, she scolded, "*I can't believe you let him in my fucking house!*"

She spewed venom at both of us. Dad didn't react at all—he was probably well used to this kind of behavior. I likewise refused to react, not getting out of my chair. This was my father's house, too, and he had invited me in. I wasn't going to let this woman get between us.

She was my father's secret—a kept woman of more than forty years and the mother of his illegitimate second family. This was the first time I had had the pleasure of meeting her, and she was certainly making an impression. Just showing up to see my father had sent her into a rage of vile accusations, threats, and verbal abuse—and that was before she assaulted me and got the cops involved.

When I left that day, my relationship with my father was permanently damaged. I had tried not to let the truth of his lies and betrayal drive us apart, even though it hurt me and even though I saw how badly it hurt my mother. I tried to maintain a connection with him, despite the ugliness of his actions. But after that day, things were never the same.

This was a man who was my hero and best friend growing up. I never would have suspected that to him we were, at best, accessories, and at worst, impediments to his life. We were ultimately expendable, as he proved through the choices he made when the truth came out.

Looking back now, there were always red flags—signs that my father was not the man we thought he was: his absences on holidays, his secrecy, and the constant excuses that took him out of town. For my mother, the signs were even stronger. She sees them now, clear as day, but at the time, she didn't pay them much thought. When you trust someone, as she trusted my father, these kinds of red flags are easy to miss or explain away. It's human nature to trust the people we love. That's what makes my father's betrayal so heinous. He took advantage of the trust that the people who loved him invested in him.

It wasn't simply infidelity. A lot of families have to deal with that type of betrayal. No, my father's deceit went far beyond sex. Through his selfish, sociopathic behavior, my father built all of our lives around a massive lie—a lie about who we were and what we meant to him. Our entire identity as a family was built upon and designed to facilitate my father's lie. The truth, when we finally learned it, not only fundamentally changed our family moving forward, it tainted every memory we had together.

My mother, through all her anguish, has urged my brother and me to find a way to move past this. "Don't let this ruin your life," she says. But unfortunately, the truth has been anything but easy to accept. While I have now found my way through the darkness, the truth my father concealed from us all these years dragged me into a deep hole and extracted a hefty toll. For my brother, who's always had a more fraught relationship with my father, it has been even harder. For him, the truth has hardened into bitter resentment and anger.

In a lot of ways, my relationship with my father made it harder for me to accept the truth but easier to have some empathy for the man. He was my best friend, and though he was never a good role model—absent to my brother and elusive to me—I valued our relationship. I wanted to understand him and his decisions even after they had caused me and our family so much pain, although that was not possible for my brother, given their poor relationship. I now believe that the lies my father hid all those years caused him to put a wall between himself and my brother. The emotional commitment to me was probably already more than he could handle. After all, he had a whole other secret family, complete with a second set of children to care about.

I cannot understate how deeply finding out the truth about my father's deceit impacted my family. But what's more evident to me, now that I can look back with more clarity, is that the lie impacted us long before the truth ever did. His absence and non-committal nature toward women and family led my brother and me down a similar path as his. In fact, all three of my father's sons were single into their forties. I treated my relationships with women as disposable and avoided commitment. This was not just a product of observing his behavior but also a consequence of growing up with his absence, which I believe left a hole inside of us that made it very hard to connect with and trust people.

By my early 40s, I was on a self-destructive path of selfish indulgence and emotional avoidance. While I always maintained my professional responsibilities, my social life was a hedonistic blur better fitted for a college student than a middle-aged man. I don't know where the path I was on would have led me but I am certain it was nowhere good.

However, while it was the consequences of my father's hidden lie that had led me to that path, it was the truth that ultimately set me free. If not for the truth, I might not be here today. I probably wouldn't have my son, who I truly believe saved my life. While the truth caused an immense amount of damage, it put me on a journey of growth and healing. But before I could begin that journey, the life I was living had to come to an end.

This is the story of how my father's lie unraveled, the harm it caused to the people involved, and my struggle to overcome the traumatic realizations that followed. It's a story of two families built on one lie, forever linked through betrayal, infidelity, and bigamy. It's also a story of resilience, recovery, and hope.

CHAPTER 1
SOMETHING'S NOT RIGHT

I t was the Tuesday after Father's Day when my mother, shaken and confused, called to tell me she had just had the strangest conversation with my father.

My father, Norman, had always been a fisherman. It was something he got from his father, whom I remember having a large blue marlin mounted on the wall of his house. Our basement was full of equipment, and he always kept a pole and tackle in his trunk. Sometimes he would call my mother, Ann, from work on a Friday and tell her he was going fishing for the weekend. We were well accustomed to dad going fishing for 24, 36, or 48 hours at a time.

While fishing was one of his pastimes, it was also a convenient excuse.

Starting sometime in the late 90s, he supposedly began going on fishing trips with a group of friends from the car business. One of them owned an RV, and they would take off together to fish at different locations in the Midwest. This is where he allegedly was on Father's Day of 2013—fishing in Missouri with his friends. It only took one call to my mother to undo a lifetime of my father's lies.

My mother told me that my father had called to tell her he was in the hospital. He said that while he had been in Missouri, he had started to feel unwell. At that point, he claimed, he decided to drive home and went to the hospital to get checked out, where they informed him that he had suffered a stroke. "Don't worry," he assured her. "I'm okay." He insisted that she didn't need to fly out to see him.

Well, that story just didn't hold water. My mother is a sharp, savvy woman, and though she had always trusted my father and never scrutinized his alibis, his story was just unbelievable. He really expected her to believe that he had suffered a stroke in Missouri, felt unwell, then drove himself six hours home before seeking medical attention. If he had been feeling unwell, why wouldn't he have sought medical treatment in Missouri? How did he drive home if he'd taken an RV with friends? Did they return with him? That, combined with how adamant he was that none of us should come to see him, was enough to raise my mother's suspicions. The story he'd told her just didn't make sense. After several strange conversations regarding my father's story, my mom decided to call the hospital to speak with a nurse.

My mother told me that she had felt something wasn't right, so she called the hospital to see if she could find out more information about his condition. On the phone, she identified herself as Norman Zimmerman's wife, to which the nurse casually replied, "Oh, I just met you and your daughter." My mother was obviously confused by this comment, as she was not there and did not have a daughter. "I'm sorry, you must be mistaken. I've never—". There was an awkward silence, and then the nurse hung up on her.

The story seemed strange, but I assumed there was some sort of miscommunication or a case of mistaken identity. I told my mother that I would call the hospital and see what I could find out. So, I called Northwestern Memorial Hospital in Chicago and got ahold of the nurse's station. "Hey, I'm Norm Zimmerman's son. I live in Philadelphia. I am just calling to check on him. Is there anything you can tell me about his condition?" I asked.

The nurse was an open book. She told me that he was doing well and that he had checked in that Monday for an elective heart valve replacement. She informed me that during the surgery, he had experienced some complications and suffered a few mild strokes, which seemed to have affected one of his legs but not his cognitive functioning. She told me that he was going to be okay.

This was interesting information. We had known that he needed a heart valve replacement for some time. He also had a condition that was causing the ball of his hip to deteriorate, which meant that he needed a hip replacement, but they were unable to do the surgery because of the heart valve issue. While the heart valve wasn't bad enough to warrant surgery by itself, if he wanted a new hip, he had to get his heart fixed first.

So, while we knew that he was thinking about getting this procedure done, he had not given us any indication that he was going to do it. He had told my mother that he was going away on a fishing trip. This didn't make any sense—why would he choose to do this in secret?

I told the nurse that I was far away and just wanted to make sure someone was there with him. She told me, "Oh, your mother, your sister, and her baby are with him."

What was she talking about? Why had he lied to us about this surgery? Who were these people with my father? Sister? Baby?

I had a hundred questions racing through my head, but I pushed them aside and simply replied, "Oh, that's not my mother, but thank you. I'm glad someone is there with him."

I hung up and called my mother back. My conversation with the hospital added to our confusion and fueled more suspicion. I didn't know what to think at that point, but it was clear that something wasn't right. I had no idea how our lives were about to change.

CHAPTER 2

UNRAVELING A LIE

My father had a history of infidelity.

One day in the spring of 1995, my mother received a knock on her door and found a man and his son standing on her stoop. The man told her, "I just want to let you know that your husband is having an affair with my wife." He then handed her an envelope full of photographic proof and details of the affair.

It turns out the man was the estranged husband of a woman named Molly who worked for my father at the car dealership. I knew Molly from when I worked at the dealership during my summers when I was younger. She had always been friendly to me but never in a way that suggested anything inappropriate. Little did I know, she was having an affair with my dad.

She'd had a child when she was young and was estranged from her son's father, but he was still concerned about her and what was going on between her and my father. Turns out, he had hired a private investigator to follow my father around, and he got a bunch of pictures of him coming and going from Molly's apartment and of them kissing at the entrance to her building.

My mother took the envelope of evidence from Molly's ex. She confronted my father about it and tried to work it out with him. That event, however, would eventually lead to her asking for a separation.

In the summer of 2013, as my mother and I started putting together the pieces from our respective phone calls to Northwestern Memorial Hospital that day in June, it didn't take long for us to start imagining what had probably happened: my father must've been screwing around again at some point and got someone pregnant.

After the initial shock and disbelief subsided, we went right to the internet to see what we could find by searching for my father's name. There are a ton of websites that specialize in this, where you can enter a person's name and they'll provide you with any publicly available details about that person. They also usually list other names that are somehow affiliated with the person. When we searched for "Norm Zimmerman," we kept seeing my name, my mother's name, and my brother's name— no surprise. But another name kept showing up as well: Margaret Zimmerman. *Was she a relative we didn't know?* We couldn't figure out who this Zimmerman was.

We did some more digging, searching on more sites, searching for Margaret's name, and looking on social media, but we weren't finding answers. That's when my mother went into her files and dug out the envelope she'd been given 18 years earlier, documenting my father's affair with Molly. Inside the envelope was the name and number of the PI who'd gathered the evidence. "Let's call him. He already knows a lot about your father," she suggested.

I called the PI, told him who I was, and refreshed him on the details of the case he had worked on regarding my father in 1995. At first, he wasn't sure, but after I gave him some details, he did remember my father. I then explained the current situation with my father, his lies, and the situation with this Margaret Zimmerman.

He offered to take the case and requested that we send him $1,000 for spending cash to start his investigation. We sent him the money the next day.

Over the next week or so, while the PI was off doing his thing, we continued to pour over the internet, trying to find any details we could about him or Margaret Zimmerman. My father, meanwhile, was still in the hospital, and my mother was maintaining daily conversations with him. Despite the emotions she was struggling with, she managed to stay calm and play it cool; we didn't want to tip him off that we were suspicious. There was also concern that confronting him could cause him to have another stroke.

My father told us that he was going to be in the hospital for another couple of weeks for rehab. He would say stuff like, "I'm fine. You guys don't need to come here. No need to fly out over this. I'm okay." We let him believe we were placated.

When we spoke to the PI the following week, he confirmed what we had already put together: My father had a secret second family.

We were able to determine that he had two children with this woman, Margaret, named Carolyn and John. We had discovered John's birthday, which informed us that my father had been involved with this woman as far back as the 60s. She wasn't just some affair he'd had or someone he'd met after he and my mother had separated; she had been in his life all along. More shocking still, I wasn't even his firstborn. His true firstborn son, John, was born 14 months before me.

The PI found that my father had numerous addresses on file where he had hidden Margaret over the years, in the suburbs of Morton Grove, Glenview, and eventually Lake Forest. He was also able to produce tax documents, boat licenses, and a bunch of other artifacts from my father's second life. It was conclusive, damning proof.

We were blown away. When something so devastating hits you so unexpectedly, it doesn't feel real at first. There's this sense of disbelief that follows. The true impact of such a blow takes a while to sink in. At that point, we were still stunned.

Faced with the undeniable truth, my mother decided to file for divorce. In retrospect, we all agree we should have gotten on a plane, gone to the hospital, and confronted him then and there, in person—but we were afraid. We weren't sure about his health, and we didn't want to cause him any stress that could worsen his condition. We were, of course, concerned because we cared about him. But there was also an awareness of how massive his lie was, and if he died, we may not have gotten any answers.

He had always told my mother, "If anything happens to me, you get everything." My mother had always taken him at his word. She knew nothing of finances or his estate planning. Now, she was suddenly faced with a grim truth: her husband had been lying to her from the start, and that meant she couldn't count on any of the promises he had made.

The truth was my father had built two separate worlds, complete with separate finances and separate insurance policies. If he had died without being exposed, we probably never would have known about any of it.

CHAPTER 3

NORMAN ZIMMERMAN, MY FATHER AND BEST FRIEND

G rowing up, I had a pretty good relationship with my father. He might not have been around as much as we would've liked, but his presence in our lives was a constant. He coached our little league teams and was involved with our Boy Scouts troop. Those things were always important to my father and he made an effort to be involved. He also encouraged us to play musical instruments, play sports, and take our academic pursuits seriously. He was at work a lot, or so we thought, so he wasn't always there to teach us right from wrong, but he was around enough to intercede if we needed it.

I admired my father in many ways. He was always taking us to baseball games, especially to see the Cubs, which had been his team his entire life. It was a legacy he passed on to me, whereas my younger brother Alan, who had a more strained relationship with my dad, became a White Sox fan—perhaps a subtle rebellion on his part. While we did go to some White Sox games for Alan, it was nowhere near as often as we would see the Cubs.

As far as I was concerned, our lives were pretty typical. Dad was working a lot, but that seemed normal to me. I was just a kid and I had no reason to suspect any part of my life wasn't normal. My father's absences were accepted as normal because I had no reason to ever suspect otherwise. Dad was a busy man with many responsibilities, and I always assumed his being gone a lot was because he was busy working hard to provide for us.

We lived in the village of Winnetka, which at that time was the most affluent Chicago suburb. It was a picturesque enclave of wealthy professionals and powerbrokers, located some twenty miles from the city's downtown. It was and remains the crown jewel of the North Shore, boasting grand homes, lush green parks, and some of the best schools in the area. It was, in many ways, the quintessential wealthy American suburb, serving as a backdrop for Hollywood hits like *Home Alone, Ferris Bueller's Day Off,* and *Uncle Buck. Caddyshack,* too, was inspired by North Shore native Bill Murray's caddying days as a youth at the Indian Hills Country Club.

My classmates' fathers were partners at McKinsey Consulting or elite law firms like Katten Muchin, CEOs of companies like Ghirardelli Chocolate, and successful plastic surgeons or cardiologists. The affluence translated to big houses, country club memberships, well-dressed families, teenagers being handed keys to their own car upon getting their driver's license, expensive vacations, and access to just about anything, good or bad. Families sent their kids to the local clothing store, Fell Company, to pick up the latest Ralph Lauren rugby and polo shirts. Materialism was rampant among Winnetka's citizens, making it the epitome of WASPy opulence. I am not saying this with a negative connotation, but rather just that it was part of the culture.

Some families had more modest means but lived in Winnetka for the sake of their kids attending terrific, high-rated schools. That privilege translated to a childhood experience that was full of access. Access to great schools, park district sports, local tennis courts and golf courses, a hockey rink, baseball and soccer fields, and even lacrosse teams, which in the 1980s was still very much an east coast sport. Kids had two Boy Scout troops from which to choose, one of which was run by the local sporting goods retailer who outfitted the scouts in all the best modern gear and equipment.

Crime was almost nonexistent in the area. Lives revolved around high-powered careers, the volunteer work of housewives, and the athletic and scholastic success of stressed-out kids trying to keep up with the fierce competition among their classmates. Winnetka always seemed safe, steady, and sane. Perhaps that is my naive recollection, or the adults just did a good job making things appear mostly perfect. It was not a town where the problems I saw on TV seemed to exist. Broken homes, scandals, domestic abuse, unemployment, organized crime, or substance abuse did not plague the residents.

My childhood home was at the center of Winnetka's privilege, on Ash Street, surrounded by wealthy attorneys, physicians, and business owners. My brother and I fit right in with the other kids our age from the block, and we remained a tight-knit group through junior high and the iconic New Trier High School. New Trier was a high-achieving pressure cooker of almost 4,000 students that funneled well-to-do kids from the five North Shore suburbs. We had an incredibly fortunate and comfortable upbringing. I didn't truly understand the privilege I enjoyed until I got to college and had an opportunity to get to know people from other backgrounds. As a boy, I thought it was all fairly typical, but I did understand that my dad had to work a lot.

Financial privilege aside, I felt my upbringing was mostly unremarkable in the sense that I perceived it to be a normal, scandal-free existence. In my youthful eyes, my parents were not involved in any wrongdoings. Mom was heavily involved in the community. Dad worked hard, ran a successful business, and operated from what appeared to be a conservative approach to parenting. I was aware of the incidents that touched other families in our community, such as the occasional DUI, somebody's dad laid off from a corporate job, divorces you would not have expected, and occasionally someone's older sibling getting in trouble while at college—what most would consider run-of-the-mill life. However, those situations never seeped into or manifested themselves in our family. About the worst thing we encountered was the serious accident I was in as a teenager when I was thrown from a vehicle in which I was a seatbeltless passenger. I had a long recovery but I came out of it without long-term side effects. Otherwise, how was I to know there was anything remarkable about my life? In no way, shape, or form did I expect that we were victims of extreme deception for forty years.

My father owned the local Schaumburg Lincoln-Mercury dealership, an operation he took over from his father. He spent a lot of time down at the car store, even when it was closed because there was always paperwork that he said he needed to catch up on. It was a place I was fond of from an early age.

As early as six years old, I would go with him to the dealership on Sundays. That was back in the 70s before Illinois passed a law that restricted dealerships from being open on Sundays because they were giving quotes to customers when the banks were closed. I always loved being there with him; I had a real affection for the place. I loved cars and the shop always had that new car smell. All the employees were nice to me, especially the old-timers that had worked for my grandfather. And I got to see my dad in his element. All these employees and all these families buying cars, and at the center of it all was my dad.

Eventually, the law changed and our Sunday workdays had to end. I would later learn that this would provide my father with the perfect alibi for his deceptions. But at the time, I was just saddened to lose that weekly ritual with my dad.

My fondness for the dealership eventually led to my working there. My first job there, however, wasn't exactly great. It was the summer after my freshman year of college, and I took a job washing cars. It was an awful job because you were outside in the summer heat, on asphalt, washing cars all day. That's all it was—just washing cars in the heat and then shuffling them around on the lot. The used car manager would come out and give us instructions in the morning on which cars to put out front by the road.

It wasn't all bad, though. At about 11 am, my dad would come into the office, and around 11:30, the woman in the front office would call me in over the P.A. system to order lunch. Then I would get to eat my lunch and hang out with the folks in the office and sometimes my father.

I also came home during Christmas break in college because I would usually have a month or so off between semesters. That's when I started working in the parts department as a delivery driver. The dealership only stocked a limited parts inventory, so all the Lincoln, Mercury, and Ford dealerships would trade parts as needed. It was my job to deliver or pick up the parts. This was a better job than washing cars. I got to hang out in the parts department with the mechanics, which allowed me to learn a little bit about how everything operated there.

Then, in the summer of 1994, I worked at the dealership full-time, selling cars from May to October. This role was on the sales floor, interacting with customers and working with the floor managers.

I was able to work with and spend more time with my father, as well. I really enjoyed spending that time with him and learning about all these different aspects of the business. On some nights, we were there late together. The showroom floor was open until 9 o'clock on weekdays, so we would order dinner and hang out in the waiting room together while the cars were being prepped after sales were closed. We watched reruns of sitcoms my father loved like *Married with Children* (ironically, a show about a man who resents his wife and family). I remember one night in 1994, the broadcast cut over to coverage of the now-infamous O.J. Simpson police chase in his white Bronco. We watched that unfold together as we ate our dinner.

I have a lot of fond memories of the dealership and of working with my father. In retrospect, it would have been a wise and logical career move for me to get into the car business as well. I certainly would've made more money owning my own dealership than I have from my career in finance. But my father never pushed me or my brother to get into the business, which is odd from the standpoint that most dealerships are family operations. That's because owning multiple dealerships is a lot of work and there's a lot of money involved, so you need someone you can trust to operate them. By keeping it in the family, it's easier to make sure no one is skimming off the top.

Typically, a family will start with one dealership and then expand from there. What's notable about my father was his disinterest in expansion or having us involved in any long-term position. My dad's dealership was located on a strip of dealerships, and over the years almost every one of them changed hands or sold to new owners. If my father had been so inclined, he could have absorbed a couple of those dealerships and expanded the business. My brother and I could've had our own stores and we all would've benefited greatly.

My father never pursued any of that. In fact, he had taken some considerable steps to limit the involvement of others in the business over the years, including his brother. From everything we've been able to piece together, it seems as if he pushed his brother out of the business by acting as his father's attorney.

At the time, none of us gave any of this much thought. But looking back, it's clear that my father kept the business to himself deliberately because it allowed him to facilitate a double life full of lies and betrayal. Allowing any of us to be a major part of that would have jeopardized his lifestyle and risked exposing him.

Work was a piece of my father's life that I only got a small glimpse of, and that was very much by design. But outside of work, he was an active father—to the point where it is almost inconceivable how he managed to be that present while also maintaining a secret second life. He and my mother would travel often, sometimes once a year with Ford Motor Company. He was actively involved in all of my and my brother's activities and pursuits: Scouts, sports, school picnics, the Pinewood Derby, etc. He spent a lot of time with us in Savanna, IL, at my mother's parents' house as well. He was, by all our accounts, a normal family man who was devoted to us.

While he may have been outside the house a lot, he was by no means an absentee father. He did stuff with us constantly. As I mentioned, taking us to major sporting events was very common. There were several Christmas Day Bulls games during the Michael Jordan era. We attended NBA Finals Game 3 in Chicago as the Bulls hosted the Utah Jazz. He even separately took me and my brother to see the Super Bowl—my brother in 1992 in Minneapolis, and me in 1995 in Miami. As kids, we attended almost every Blackhawks playoff game, which was quite a few games. Then there was the 2003 MLB

All-Star game in Chicago. Finally, an annual tradition throughout the 1980s was a weekend trip to my father's alma mater, the University of Illinois, for a football game. I have vivid memories of my father's joy in seeing the 1983 Illini have a great season, which resulted in a Rose Bowl appearance. We sat in the end zone that fall when Illinois rallied to beat Ohio State, 17-13.

All that added to what seemed like a normal childhood. We lived in a very affluent community of business professionals, where other dads were always traveling for business, so it didn't seem odd that my dad wasn't always around. And from my mother's perspective, her life was quite comparable to the other wives in the area. As such, she accepted our lives as normal. My mother was extremely loyal and loved my father very much, and as a child, I accepted what she accepted as normal.

My father was my best friend and my role model. I never suspected he had secrets that he kept from us. His behavior always seemed genuine. His affection was never questioned. None of us had any reason to suspect otherwise. It's important to understand this to understand how deeply the truth both shocked and hurt us. It was not at all a case of knowing something was wrong for years only to have our suspicions confirmed. Instead, we blissfully resided in the false reality he had created for us, believing our lives and our relationship with him were normal and even ideal.

And it's important to emphasize that for all his flaws and betrayal, there was some part of him that was a caring father and husband—a part of him that did his best to be what we thought he was. That's what makes the truth so hard to comprehend. If my father had been a lousy, shitty person to us at home, it would have been easier to accept his betrayals. Instead, the truth left us unable to reconcile the man we thought we knew with the terribly hurtful and inconsiderate choices he made.

My father was my best friend. He's also the person who hurt me more than anyone else ever could. That's the complex truth that I still struggle with today.

CHAPTER 4
ANN "BOUSEMAN" ZIMMERMAN

My mother, Ann Bouseman, grew up in Savanna, Illinois, a small town on the Mississippi River about three hours west of Chicago. Her father was a yardmaster for Burlington Northern Railroad, where he worked the night shift. He had gone to college on a track scholarship but dropped out during the Great Depression to help his family on their farm. Her mother was a very intelligent woman but grew up dirt poor as one of thirteen children.

Together, Tom and Katherine Bouseman raised livestock and farmed on a small scale for their personal use. They had about 25 acres of farmland, hills, and woods. Savanna was a beautiful little place that I used to look forward to visiting as a child. I adored my mother's parents, and spending time in Savanna is one of my most treasured memories. Savanna could not be more different than Winnetka, and that was probably much of the allure I felt for my visits there. From the time I was a toddler, I would go visit my grandparents, and all through my childhood until 1983 when my grandparents moved to Arkansas to escape the cold snowy Western Illinois winters, I spent a ton of time in Savanna.

Both my mother's parents were aware that their circumstances had limited their potential. As such, the education of their two children was very important to them and they had high expectations for both. Their son—my uncle—was valedictorian of his class and went on to be a well-known etymologist at the University of Illinois and Illinois Natural History Survey, and even though it wasn't common for women to go to college at the time, my mother was always expected to.

My mother was smart, attractive, and ambitious, and she couldn't get out of Savanna soon enough. She was a National Merit Scholar, which opened the door for her to attend Bradley University in Peoria. From there, she was off to Chicago with dreams of becoming an architect. Unfortunately, in the early 60s, that was an industry that was not really open to women. She was forced to settle for working at an architecture firm and eventually in the office design and supply industry. She did that for some time and would eventually go on to start her own company, which she successfully ran for twenty years.

In 1963, she was set up on a blind date with my father. He was a young attorney in Chicago at the time, living at home with his parents. My father was witty, funny, and charming. Always had great stories. He was also a good-looking guy who always dressed well. The two of them hit it off and they dated for four years, which was a long time, even then. Now we know why my father was dragging things out: he was involved with Margaret. My mother, bless her heart, would have never suspected such deceit.

The two of them came from completely different worlds. Mom was from a small town and her life was very much rural Americana. She came from a line of big families who didn't have much. Her family line stretched back to the Pennsylvania Dutch during the American Revolution. Dad, on the other hand, was the child of immigrants—

his mother's family fled Russia when she was only two years old and his father's family came from Hungary—and he grew up in a rough neighborhood in Chicago. As such, Dad was more street savvy and less trusting of people. He understood exactly how dishonest the world was and had no problem partaking in it to his benefit. Mom was naïve and trusting. When she came to the big city, she met my father and he became her world.

Finally, after four years of dating, my mother gave him an ultimatum and he gave in and married her. Their engagement spurred a last-minute move of their wedding date, which we now understand was probably his attempt to better position himself to juggle his relationship with Margaret and marry my mother. They were finally married in 1967, but I wasn't born for four more years. Again, for the time, this was peculiar. My dad was 35 and my mother was 31 when I was born, which made them older first-time parents in that era.

My parents were married on December 8, 1967, in the study of Rabbi Alan Tarshish in Glencoe. It was a Jewish ceremony, and my mom agreed that any offspring would be brought up in the faith. Attendees at the wedding were Tom & Kathryne Bouseman (my mom's parents), Bill and Ann Zimmerman (my dad's parents), and Paul & Jeanne Zimmerman (My dad's brother and sister-in-law). John & Barbara Bouseman were supposed to attend but were ill and did not make the trip. They had a champagne luncheon following the ceremony at the Belden Stratford Hotel in Lincoln Park, Chicago. Other friends and family who were there: Norm's aunt Miriam Applebaum and her husband; Aunt Goldie Saccharin; Uncle Bennie and Sylvia Saccharin from Memphis; Laddie & Jackie Votanek (my mom's employer); Bridget and Sheldon Becker; Jim Adelman; and Jerry Hechman. There are very few photos from the big day as Tom

Bouseman, a great dad but not a great photographer, kept forgetting to take pictures. The wedding was very low-key.

The wedding was kept very small at the request of the groom. You can tell by the attendees that it was very one-sided. My dad was running the show even then. He did not want a lot of people there, so none of my mom's friends were there except Bridget. I think even then he had secrets that had to be protected. No one from his legal world was there.

They were married on a Friday morning, and after the luncheon, they drove to Lake Geneva and spent the weekend at the Abbey. They returned on Sunday, and stopped by his parents' home at 5300 North Virginia, Chicago, to pick up some of his clothes and belongings. They then returned to my mom's apartment at 509 Barry, Chicago. Both returned to their offices on Monday morning.

My father was hesitant and generally unenthused about every step of their relationship. When my mother told him she was pregnant with me, it was no different. She recalls that he just wasn't excited, especially for a first-time father. Now we know that he'd just had a son with Margaret 14 months earlier, and the reality of his situation was probably sinking in. He was stuck.

I assume that Margaret's pregnancy was an accident. He got her pregnant, and between the social attitudes of the time and her Catholic faith, there was no way she was getting an abortion. Rather than doing the honorable thing—coming clean and divorcing my mother—my father decided to stay with both women. Margaret then had John in March of 1970, and later that year, he discovered my mother was pregnant.

That Thanksgiving, my father was unexpectedly called away from home for a business trip, leaving my mother home alone and pregnant. When he returned, he told her that the airline had lost his luggage. We now believe that this is when my father took Margaret away and married her in a sham union that was not legally binding. His luggage probably went back home with her along with keepsakes from the trip.

This marriage, which my father would later insist to my mother and me was a sham, satisfied Margaret and her Catholic family's belief that she should be married to the father of her child. None of them knew that Norm Zimmerman was already married in the state of Illinois. There were no electronic records back then; no way for anyone to check.

To the day he died, my father insisted he wasn't a bigamist. This second marriage was a sham to him. But legal or not, he lived as Margaret Zimmerman's husband. She took his name. She bore his children, who were given his name. He provided for them. Insured them. He was her husband in every way that counts. He just could not bring himself to admit to that and accept the label of a bigamist. It was the lie he told himself while lying to both women.

By May of 1971 when I was born, my father was fully involved with two women, living two separate lives built on deception. It's a ruse he kept up for 42 years. And in 2013, my mother, Ann "Bouseman" Zimmerman, had to discover that her entire life with the man she loved had been a lie—that she became a stay-at-home mother to a man who cheated on her, lied to her, and kept a secret second illegitimate family. We moved from the city to Winnetka in 1973. My mom wanted us out of the city and into the suburbs, but my father did not want to move to the suburbs. He already secretly had Margaret holed up in a small house in Morton Grove. Keeping us in the city kept his worlds separate and easy, but my mom insisted we head to the suburbs. She would go out searching for homes with the realtor. At the time, the market was hot, similar to how it was in 2020-2021, and during the course of their search they lost out on 12 homes. My father would come to see the house, and then as they prepared their offers, he would write numerous contingencies on the back of the contract. Sellers would reject their offers, and the search would go on. My father was secretly hoping he would not need to buy a second home. How was this guy in his fairly young attorney's practice able to afford a house in Morton Grove, let alone another in Winnetka?! My mom said he had a strict budget in mind for the house they could buy—now we know why. Eventually, they purchased 1136 Ash St, and that was the start of what became almost 30 years of home ownership in Winnetka.

The lives they led there were very independent of one another. My father was often working, away fishing, or on his alleged business trips—or so Mom was led to believe. She was not one to sit around and watch the clock, waiting for his return, however. She lived a very independent lifestyle, especially for the time. My mother was an entrepreneur who started her own interior design business, a socialite, and an accomplished community organizer. She was the first woman to serve on the Winnetka Police and Fire Commission, and President of the Board of Governors at Winnetka Community House. Additionally, she served on the Museum Board and the Women's Board.

Of course, my mother's community involvement posed problems for my father. While I am sure he was happy that she was always occupied and not focused on what he was doing, these activities often presented opportunities for local suburban press and sometimes even the larger Chicago papers. My dad was always very cagey about appearing in pictures with my mom. He would often insist that she take the photo without him, asserting it was only fair since it was *her* accomplishment. One time the Chicago Tribune wanted to get a picture of my mother, the other members of the board, and their families. My father ran away in such a way that my mother was embarrassed. Of course, none of us thought much about it at the time. Now, however, it makes complete sense. He couldn't risk appearing in the paper with her. Margaret or somebody they knew might've seen it.

My mother was always a very bright, capable, and independent person. She trusted my father and went about living her life. Forty-six years of marriage later, when the truth was finally revealed, I am sure that many of those memories played back for her. The pattern of behavior could be so well explained by something none of us ever would have dreamed possible. Infidelity was one thing—and that was bad enough—but to have an entire second family hidden away in a nearby suburb? It still feels like something out of a movie rather than real life.

Forty-six years of lies and deceit. Not only had my father been lying to her, but she had also essentially been forced to live a lie as well. For nearly half a century, she was allowed to believe her life was something it wasn't. Even though discovering the truth had left her understandably shocked, she knew she had to file for divorce. There was no doubt in her mind that this was the right thing to do. This presented a dilemma: she didn't want to cause him stress by serving him at the hospital, but once he was back home, serving him with divorce papers might have been impossible. He could have found ways to evade the process server. Given this consideration, we decided it was best to serve him while he was still in the hospital.

The first call he made after being served with the papers was to me. "Mike, it's dad."

I knew exactly why he was calling but played it cool. "Hey, dad. How's it going?"

"Did you know your mother was going to serve me with divorce papers?" he asked me.

"Yes, I did know that," I said calmly.

"*Why?*"

"Well, because we found out you have another life with a secret family."

There was a brief pause, and then he simply said, "Oh… Okay… I guess I better call your mother now."

About an hour later, my mother called me. "I just got off the phone with your father," she said.

I asked her how it went and she recounted their conversation. She had confronted him and he was very non-committal about everything. He said, "Okay, well, I guess there's going to be some revelations." All in all, he kept everything at a high level and was very matter-of-fact about things. "How much money do you want?" he asked her bluntly. After 46 years, this was all he had to say to her.

"I don't know," she told him. "I don't know how much money you have."

He then said something we found strange. "I guess this is the end of my relationship with the boys," he said.

"That's up to you," she replied.

The conversation was unsettling for both of us. This man that we thought we knew so well was acting so callous and with such disregard. It was sociopathic behavior—there was no grief, no regret, and no concern for the damage he had caused. He was preparing to cut us out of his life just like that.

We couldn't wrap our heads around the second part. What did he mean by his relationship with me and my brother being over? Why would he think that? Did he think we wouldn't want to have a relationship with him? Or was it something else?

Ultimately, we found out. It was something else: it was Margaret. He knew that now that the truth was out, he had the risk of us exposing him to his secret world, so he would need to cut ties with us. In addition, he knew she would never allow him to have a relationship with us.

CHAPTER 5
A HISTORY OF LIES

In 1989, my father was diagnosed with polycythemia vera, a type of blood cancer. When I learned of this news, I was away attending my freshman year at the University of Rochester. It was just before Thanksgiving break, and I was eagerly looking forward to going home and seeing my family. Those first few months away from home had seemed like an eternity as I navigated the challenges and adjustments that accompany such major life changes. While I was adapting well to my new city, running on the cross-country team, taking challenging classes, rushing fraternities, forging new friendships, and even being elected to student government, there was still that longing for home and family. My father's diagnosis, however, would make the reunion less than ideal.

Just before I was to fly home for the long weekend, my mom called to tell me my father was in the hospital from a ruptured blood vessel, which had burst in his intestines. As a result, he had to have part of his intestines removed. The blood disease he was diagnosed with caused his body to produce too many red platelets, which leads to blood clots. The condition had caused a clot that led to the burst vessel in his intestines. So, upon arriving home for Thanksgiving break, our weekend was spent visiting my dad in the hospital.

As we learned, my dad's disease would require lifelong treatment. Initially, he was told that the typical life expectancy for someone with the disease was 7-12 years. Learning that cast a pall over us, as my dad was only 53 at the time. He continued to go for regular red blood tests every few weeks to monitor his red blood cell counts, and the doctor would take blood to manage his levels. Eventually, he ended up on medicines to help manage his levels. The doctor indicated there were some concerns about the long-term side effects of medication, and my father frequently complained that it sapped his energy. Of course, none of us could predict he would go on to live for several more decades.

Once I had learned of my dad's double life, I came to doubt some of his claims. I do not doubt his claim about his blood disease, as that has been verified in court proceedings; however, his claims about his diminished energy levels and fatigue were questionable. He also claimed the medicine made him impotent; however, that claim is dubious as well. Once he was diagnosed with his disease, my mother lived in fear of his death. She often let things go and gave my dad a pass in general because she felt he was living on borrowed time. She remarked that while she was unhappy in her marriage dating back to the mid-90s, she always felt that due to his disease and short lifespan, she had no reason to go through the hardship of divorce. In retrospect, this was a strategic error. Whether it was deliberate or not, by positioning his disease as he had, it gave him additional space in his marriage in which to operate his double life. My mother did not protest his fishing trips as hard as she used to or give him as much grief about missing time with us during holidays.

The impact his looming death had on me manifested in chronic stress. I was always worried about my dad's health and longevity. Once

I was no longer living in Chicago, time spent with my dad became less frequent, but every moment we did spend together, I cherished, aware that it was limited. I made an effort to call him on the phone more, which was never really a chore. I loved our conversations—we would chat for hours about sports, politics, my work life, my dating life, and more.

I look back and marvel that over all those years he never slipped up with details or topics between his two worlds and families. Although, as we learned, the vast majority of his time was spent with us, his legal family. Still, I am amazed at how he kept it all straight—two sets of details, stories, and lies—all while running a large business. That had to be stressful. It's enough to make you wonder if it contributed to him getting sick.

In 1996, one year after my father's affair with Molly was discovered, my mother finally asked him for a separation. However, my parents remained close and civil for the sake of our family. They spoke daily and always maintained a civilized relationship. It was at that time that my father got his own apartment near the car dealership. He would split his time between the apartment and the home he owned with Margaret. Despite being separated from my mother, he continued to see Margaret only occasionally; he was not going to deviate from the established norm by spending more time with her. After all, she and her kids thought he was a busy attorney. He couldn't just start being home all the time. The apartment gave my father a place to live that was not with Margaret. It also served, as we later found out, as a destination for years' worth of birthday, Christmas, and Father's Day presents we gave to my dad, which he could not bring into his home with Margaret. His double life required him to maintain the same appearance all the time regardless of where he traveled.

There were days in which he saw both families, so he had to maintain identical double wardrobes from the same clothing manufacturers. He kept it simple: generally dark blue or gray suits with white, button-down collared shirts. He wore the same black, leather, slip-on dress shoes year after year. The same dark polyester slacks and dark blue or burgundy V-neck sweaters year after year. The same boring short-sleeved, button-down, plaid shirts in bland dark patterns. He owned at most two pairs of blue jeans, which were only worn for fishing, boy scout trips, or when coaching our softball or baseball games.

This setup ensured that he could always come and go as he pleased in either circumstance. However, once his secret was out and my mother had served him with divorce papers, things quickly changed. From his perspective, he was no longer able to deny the truth. And until that point, he was free to come and go whenever, wherever he liked.

Now, following his stroke and heart valve replacement in 2013, his freedom was limited. He couldn't drive anymore; his wings were forever clipped. It must have occurred to him that with his impending divorce from my mother and his health in disarray, he would be essentially stuck at Margaret's, who was not going to allow him much leeway. We later learned in conversations with Patty, his longtime office manager, who continued to work for my dad, that he openly complained about Margaret. In one conversation with Patty, he expressed regret for marrying her. He knew that was the nail in his coffin of freedom.

My mother had moved to Arizona many years earlier, but our family would still get together every summer in Chicago, usually around my brother's birthday. We would stay in hotels downtown or the suburbs, as my mom no longer had her house and dad just had the apartment—or so we thought. On those weekends, dad would leave the house he shared with Margaret to stay in the apartment so he could have the freedom to visit with us around town. I visited him under similar circumstances up until Father's Day of 2012 when we went to see a Cub's game together.

In 1998, my parents went on a Ford Motor Company trip to Arizona, and my mom really enjoyed her time there. She had developed asthma in her older age, but in Arizona, she noticed the dry air helped her symptoms subside. Her doctor told her that Arizona would be a good place for her to live and feel better. Once my mom expressed an interest in building a house there, my father encouraged her to pursue it. She made several more trips to Sedona, eventually buying a piece of land, and then working with an architect to build the house she would move to in 2001. It was approximately a $1M home, and shortly after that, my father also built a new $1M house for Margaret in Lake Forest, IL. He was keeping the scorecard even, at least regarding buying both unhappy women new homes.

My father would also fly out to stay with us for five days at Christmas, though he never stayed for New Year's Day. Unbeknownst to us, that's when he would return to the other family. The freedom and mobility he had enabled for himself over the years made living his lies much easier.

At the time of his stroke, my father still had the apartment, and even though the car dealership had sold the previous December, he still had some obligations at the dealership involved with winding the business down. He still had employees in his employment, and he had all remaining business records moved to his apartment, which needed to be sorted through to determine if they should be kept or destroyed.

That meant that throughout the remainder of 2013 and into 2014, he needed to be able to get to his apartment. So, he would have one of his office managers give him a ride from Margaret's or take a taxi if necessary. These excursions were the only instances where he left the house after his stroke.

It was this information that brought his comment to my mother upon being served divorce papers— "I guess this is the end of my relationship with the boys" —into focus. Under his new circumstances, he knew he would not have the ability or the freedom to see my brother and me if we were to come to town. As such, my father was prepared to sacrifice his relationship with me to continue his life with Margaret. He was elderly, in poor health, and in need of someone to take care of him, and that someone was going to have to be Margaret because she was local to him in Chicago.

Once my father's lie was exposed, the dynamic of our family quickly changed. Because he was an attorney, my father knew how to shield himself. As a result, he avoided disclosure, being careful about what he said and how much detail he shared with us, which dragged out the divorce process. We had hoped that he would do the right thing for my mother and the family now that he had been caught; we knew the other family's names, their ages, their dates of birth, and the addresses of where they had lived, among other things. The truth was irrefutable, but it quickly became apparent that my father was not going to disclose how much money he had. He put up his defenses and retreated into his shell almost immediately.

For the rest of 2013, I regularly talked to him over the phone and tried to extract any details I could about why he did what he did, how it had happened or any information about his other family. I was friendly with him, hoping that if I kept things amicable, he might open up to me. He would also occasionally talk with my mother, though he was much more guarded with her, and he continued to fight her over the divorce. My mother was still in shock from the revelation, and she stayed that way for a long time. I don't think she knew what to do or how to handle it. The whole thing left her emotionally crushed.

In November 2013, my mother was diagnosed with breast cancer. Perhaps she would have developed it either way, but she blames my father and the stress he put her through for accelerating her cancer and worsening her condition. My mother's diagnosis cast a different light on the events we had been through. When we made my father aware of her diagnosis, he seemed to show empathy, but based on my conversations with him, I determined his other family knew nothing about us or the divorce process. Until that juncture, the burden had been ours alone to shoulder.

CHAPTER 6

THE OTHER FAMILY

They deserved to know.

After my father's lies had been revealed to us on that fateful day just before Father's Day in 2013, my mother and I talked about the other family. As hurt and confused as we were, we recognized that this other family was also victimized by my father's deceit. It was only right that we let them know what we had discovered.

We also wrongly assumed that getting the other family involved would put pressure on my dad to settle with my mother in a timely manner, though this would ultimately backfire on us, leaving my father even more intransigent.

Once we'd decided to notify the other family, there was still the matter of how we would do it. It's not like we could just call this Margaret woman on the phone. We decided that a letter to the daughter, Carolyn, would be the best move.

At the local post office, I examined the innocuous envelope and wondered what kind of reaction and drama it would cause. It contained an anonymous letter stating only simple facts:

"Ann and Norman Zimmerman have been married for 47 years. They have two children, Michael and Alan, who they raised in Winnetka."

I stuck the envelope containing the letter inside a USPS express envelope and brought it to the counter to ship. I paid for overnight shipping to Chicago, where I had arranged for a friend to receive it. They would then take the letter inside, addressed it to Carolyn, and drop it in a local mailbox. That way, when Carolyn received the letter, it would have a local postmark. We wanted the other family to know the truth, but we didn't want it traced back to us, lest we provoke my father's ire.

My mother still had plenty of friends in the area, and any one of them could've known what was going on and felt compelled to speak up about it, so there was inherent deniability as long as the letter came from someone in the Chicago area.

The letter was sent around Christmas time in 2013. We spent the next week waiting for something to happen. It was only a matter of time before we heard word or received a call from someone. Sure enough, Carolyn looked up my mother on the internet and called her for answers.

My mother was very nice and accommodating to Carolyn, who was in disbelief and had a lot of questions. "This is impossible," Carolyn asserted. "My mother is such a good Catholic woman. She's been married to my father forever." She was totally in the dark. I can sympathize with her at this point because she was completely blindsided by the truth, just like I had been. My mother patiently spoke with her for about an hour, detailing her relationship and history with my father.

It became clear that there were a lot of things about my father's life of which they had been unaware. Carolyn had been told her entire life that his parents—her grandparents—were dead. In fact, my dad's mother lived until 1993. But she was never allowed to know her grandparents, and they died never knowing my father had another family. They were also not aware that he owned a car dealership—they had been told that an uncle of his owned the dealership in the 70s.

Eventually, the conversation started to include me, and Carolyn asked if she could speak to me. My mother obliged and gave her my number. I was happy to speak with her; I felt she deserved to know the truth and wanted to validate what she had learned. I also wanted to assert, without any contention or grievance, the truth of the matter: that we were my father's legitimate family. I politely peppered in details about all the Cubs and Blackhawks games we went to with him, traveling with him, visiting his parents, and so forth.

My father had worked meticulously to keep his two worlds separate. That meant making sure that there was no overlap; no possible source of exposure. For us, that meant bizarre schedules and some sketchy excuses for missing holidays. But for them, it was much more extensive. He misled them about so much; they didn't even know how he made his money. They thought he was a lawyer who had to travel a lot, which was revealing. My father hadn't practiced law in decades, yet he'd kept his law office in Chicago all those years. Now we know why: To keep the rouse up with his second family.

Carolyn was in total shock, which I understood. I had had six months to work through and process the truth, but she was just learning it and had some skepticism. But I provided her with so much information that it was irrefutable. I was able to fill in blanks for her, answering questions she'd always had about his absences, and she was able to do some of the same for me when we compared notes.

"He spent every Sunday with us," Carolyn told me.

"That's interesting," I replied. "Because the car dealership was closed on Sundays, but he would always tell my mother he had to go in and do paperwork. He'd wake up early, have breakfast, and head to work for the day."

"He would always come home late Sunday morning or early in the afternoon from traveling…" She was connecting the dots. "We would spend the day together."

"Meanwhile, he had my mother believing he was working at the dealership, which was closed, so she had no way to call him."

It was a convenient story that my mother never doubted. Why would she? But it's hard to imagine it from Carolyn's perspective— where did they think he was coming from? The more I learned, the harder it was to understand how they hadn't seen through his lies. There were so many holes in the stories he fed them.

I started to wonder how much Margaret knew. Was she complicit in my father's schemes, or perhaps willfully ignorant? Had she helped to sell the lie to their children?

I didn't share my suspicions with Carolyn. She and I talked for a while longer, sharing memories and comparing notes. There was an awkward conversation about traveling as a family, where Carolyn noted that my father had never traveled with them. I, on the other hand, had numerous detailed stories about our family trips and the time dad went to Europe with us for a 10-day high school trip. There was this uncomfortable moment where I think Carolyn was comprehending the implications of this—that *we* were my father's primary family and that they were his shameful secret kept hidden away from public view while he was out living a normal life with us.

"I don't know what I am going to do," she confided. "My brother is going to be devastated…"

I felt for her and her brother, John. I still think about John a lot. I'm sure it was hard for him to find out the truth. He was raised to believe he was my father's firstborn and only son. His childhood, from what I can ascertain, was pretty rough. When he was 5 or 6, his first sister—my father's firstborn daughter—died in infancy. The loss must've been hard for Margaret and John, and as much as I have come to believe that my father has no empathy, it had to have affected him to some degree, as well.

When I think about that period in my dad's life, it's hard to believe. In 1976, he lost both his first daughter and his father. He was dealing with his father dying of lung cancer, taking over the car business with all that entailed, and living his normal life with us. All the while, he was secretly grieving the loss of his daughter and had another family that was in mourning. How did he make time for them? It's unfathomable to understand how he could be dealing with tragic events in both of his lives at the same time and still manage to make it work—though from what I learned from Carolyn, he didn't make it work very well. There was a palatable hole from his absence in their lives; John was going to be crushed to find out why his father was never around. I am sure he and Margaret mourned the loss of that child, however, he had to carry around those emotions for all those decades. I know if I were him that I would have felt a huge sense of guilt about not being around that household enough.

I wished Carolyn well and told her to let me know if she had any other questions. I fully expected to have further conversations with her. I thought I had an ally. Who else could better relate to what I was going through? I couldn't have been more wrong.

A couple of days later, I got a voicemail from my father asking me to call him. I could hear Margaret in the background absolutely losing her mind, crying and screaming, "*I can't believe they told them! I can't believe they told our children!*"

Her reaction was very telling. It validated my suspicions: *Margaret knew!* To what extent, I am still unsure, but she must've known she wasn't the only woman and that my father had another life. Otherwise, she would have been just as confused and devastated as the rest of us. She should've been ripping pissed at my father but instead, she was mad at us. That meant she had some knowledge and had lied to her kids their whole lives.

When I spoke to my father, he was accusatory and interrogative. "Who sent the letter?" he demanded to know.

"Dad, I honestly don't know," I said, playing dumb.

"Did *you* write it?!"

"No, Dad. Mom has a lot of friends in the area and I'm sure a lot of them are mad about all this."

"Was it Susan? Or Cindy?" he interrogated, rambling off a list of my mother's friends and associates.

"I have no idea," I insisted.

"You contacted Carolyn, though," he asserted. This was just untrue but it may be what Carolyn told him. Either that or he was just lying to see what I would say.

"No, Dad, she called me."

"Well, why did you tell her so much?" he asked.

"Dad," I said, my tone trying to assuage his anger. "All I did was answer her questions. We both had questions."

"You told her too much," he retorted.

I don't know what possessed him to think that I would lie for him or carry his water. He must've assumed that because we had a close relationship, he could count on me to keep my mouth shut. In his mind, this was a matter between he and my mother, and I should stay out of it.

"I had no reason not to answer her questions."

My father was very unhappy. This had unraveled 40-some-odd years of work. I imagine that Carolyn and John had confronted them and the fallout was not pretty. Now, he was fighting a war on two fronts: the divorce battle with my mother on one and the fallout from his lies to his other family on the other.

It became clear very quickly that we had made a mistake bringing the other family into the dispute at this point. Now my father had pressure from Margaret to deal with regarding finances. She was now aware of the divorce settlement. Instead of motivating my father to settle quickly, it likely dragged out the process.

My mother tried to fight but soon grew tired. She was battling cancer and losing a lot of money in attorney fees.

"I just want this to be over," she told me in the spring of 2014.

I tried to encourage her to keep fighting. "This is what he wants. To wear you down so you have to give in."

It was a battle of attrition that he eventually won. In July 2014, she settled for less than she should have.

CHAPTER 7

LEANING ON FAITH

The infamous and unfortunate star of the Boston Red Sox's 1986 World Series team, Bill Buckner, once said, "The dreams are that you're gonna have a great series and win. The nightmares are that you're gonna let the winning run score on a ground ball through your legs. Those things happen, you know. I think a lot of it is just fate."

Bill Buckner's fate was to commit a fielding error that would become one of the most famous plays in baseball history. His entire career would be overshadowed by one major mistake made when the pressure was at its highest.

I remember when Bill's life drastically changed on that fateful day the ball rolled through his legs, allowing the winning runs to score during a decisive tenth inning, costing his team the championship. He was an elite hitter who'd played for the Cubs, and for twenty-two seasons, he had an all-star career. But his life and career were overshadowed by that one error made in the 1986 World Series against the New York Mets. In a flash, his life changed. That one moment forever defined his career and changed the trajectory of his life until his passing in 2019.

Like Buckner, my father made a lot of errors that changed the trajectory of not only his life but those of his two families. The difference, of course, was that Bill's mistake was an innocent error that many players have made over the years—just not during a critical game that led to the loss of the '86 World Series—whereas my father's "errors" were premeditated and carefully executed.

Buckner said that he leaned on his faith to get him through the tough times and that this was an example he hoped would inspire others during their own struggles.

That's where I have trouble. Faith is hard for me to lean on. As a kid, Easter was cool. Like other kids in the neighborhood, we woke up to Easter baskets with candy and some gifts. It was a fun holiday as a kid. However, the religious significance of the holiday was lost on me. We didn't practice religion at all; it never seemed important to my parents. We simply celebrated all the Christian holidays, especially those with gifts involved. The focus was more on the materialistic angle, which was part of growing up privileged and keeping up with the Joneses.

Over time, through adulthood, I grew to feel more awkward about Easter weekend. I was aware that my father was Jewish, and my mom was Christian. The agreement between my parents at marriage was when the time came, my brother Alan and I would be raised Jewish. However, that discussion and agreement were before we lived in Winnetka. Upon moving to Winnetka, their priorities shifted. The synagogue where we would join reached out to us, resulting in my mother approaching the topic with Dad. The synagogue was a reformed synagogue in Northfield, which was a neighboring suburb to Winnetka and Glenview. It drew from the surrounding area and at that point, the locality of the synagogue was problematic for my dad. It was too close to Glenview where Margaret was housed with the kids. How could we take up religion at that location and risk the overlapping of separate families and their worlds? My father mildly suggested my mom ask Alan and me what we wanted to do. After all, we knew very few Jewish kids and my mother had yet to convert from Christianity, so perhaps we would just choose the Christian faith along with our friends in Winnetka. Well, the irony of this was that my dad had a secret family with a Polish Catholic woman and was raising his illegitimate family Catholic. A detail my mother always knew from my father was that he thought Jewish women were too controlling. Interesting how he deliberately sought relationships with Christian women who were less demanding than my father's perception of their Jewish peers.

As such, Easter was always an odd holiday for us, but I always thought it was because my dad was Jewish. In reality, since Easter falls on a Sunday, he was with his other family on Easter Sundays. Since my father had my mom trained to think Easter was not a meaningful holiday to him, he would often use it as an excuse to "go fishing" that weekend. Of course, we now know those fishing trips were spent just six miles away in a neighboring suburb.

So, my dad would head off to "go fishing" on the Saturday of Easter weekend, and return late on Sunday night. Meanwhile, my mom, brother, and I would spend the day together while my father was off playing the role of a family man in his second household. My mother would take us to the Easter egg hunt at the Village Green in Winnetka, and then we would typically spend the rest of the day on a sugar high, eating chocolate bunnies and Peeps Marshmallows from the Easter baskets she'd gotten us. There was no religious aspect to our Easter traditions.

It wasn't just Easter, either: all our holidays were untraditional in some regard. Because this was all I knew, I never took it as out of the ordinary at the time. Whether it was my dad "playing cards" with other Jewish lawyers on Christmas eve or collecting rent in the Austin section of Chicago on Thanksgiving, it just became routine for us. When it came to holidays at the Zimmerman house, my father only participated for part of the day on Thanksgiving and Christmas Day. I know it bothered my mom that the duration of our holiday events always felt truncated, but my dad made use of his favorite alibi: that he needed to be at the car dealership.

I've already discussed how Carolyn and I were able to piece together my father's Thanksgiving routine based on the lies each family was told.

Christmas was even more interesting. He would spend Christmas Eve with Margaret and their children but was never there when John and Carolyn woke up on Christmas morning. For as long as I could remember, Dad supposedly played cards with some fellow Jewish attorneys every Christmas Eve. That was his surefire get-out-of-the-house-play every Christmas Eve. He would come back late from "playing cards" on Christmas Eve night and was there when Alan and I woke up in the morning to see what Santa brought us.

In our neighborhood on Ash Street, there was a Christmas Eve gathering at the Howards' house with about five families represented. The gatherings began to take on more meaning once all the kids were high school and college age, and I have fond memories of those Christmas eve gatherings. My father often started the evening there with us, and then he would slip out around 8:00 pm for his "card game," which we now know was his cover to spend Christmas Eve with the other family.

The interesting wrinkle was that dad was there with us at our house on Christmas morning. He spent part of his night with

Margaret and their kids, then came home around 3 am to our house. *What could he possibly have arranged with Margaret to never spend Christmas with them?* Margaret and her family were Catholic, so they celebrated Christmas.

My dad then spent all day with us until his mother and my cousin Diane joined us for Christmas dinner.

The story Carolyn eventually told me was that they always thought Dad was going to Florida to visit his old college friend, Sheldon Becker. Come to find out, Shelly Becker did not move to Florida until around 1990. For all those years Margaret and their kids believed he was leaving them in the middle of the night to fly to Florida, the truth was that he was actually in Winnetka with us, just shy of seven miles away.

Remarkably, Dad pulled that stunt each Christmas for over forty years. My dad was not around enough during the holidays, and I had always wished he had been. Since he was Jewish, I just always assumed Christmas was not as important to him as it was to my mother. As a kid, it was easy to justify that to myself. However, as an adult, it makes no sense. Regardless of my father's childhood religious upbringing, he should have been a much greater part of our holidays.

However, the holidays were likely always a burden to him. Giving him gifts was always fascinating because he was impossible to buy for. He kept identical sets of clothes at both homes. He had to—he could not risk showing up at one house or the other wearing something that had not come from the collection of clothes within each respective home—the same colors, brands, styles, etc. He would leave our house in the morning and sometimes visit the other house during the course of the day before returning to our house in the evening. So, if we got him a gift like a shirt or a sweater, we were actually complicating his life. He would then need to remember which house it belonged to. Most clothing gifts were returned because he would find something wrong with the fit of the item. What a guy—more concerned about covering his ass than keeping gifts from his kids. It was not until much later in life, once he had his own apartment that he suddenly had a place to hide all the gifts we gave him.

There were years when we would travel to my grandparents' home in western Illinois during Christmas break that always felt much more like what Christmas was supposed to feel like. On my grandparents' 25-acre property, they had a field of fir trees where people could come cut down their own Christmas trees. My grandparents made a few bucks off the sale of those trees but it was cool to see families coming out to find their perfect tree. Many of them seemed to have something we didn't.

It was really how my grandparents decorated their house for the holidays that made it feel the way I thought Christmas was supposed to be. My grandfather built the house in the late 1940s, over a year and a half. It was such a neat place to visit. While there was a furnace, my grandparents supplemented heating with two wood-burning stoves, one of which was in the kitchen/family room. My grandfather spent the summer and fall chopping wood to heat the house during those cold Midwest winters that swept down from Canada and the Dakotas. At Christmas, their house would typically have not just one, but three to four Christmas trees decorated, along with ample fir boughs throughout the house. Going to Grandma and Grandpa Bouseman's house for the holidays was special. Add to it that my grandmother was a fabulous cook, and there were always tons of wonderful baked goods to enjoy. My father would sometimes join us on our trips out to Savanna, IL, but most years he was not able to get away from work. In retrospect, our trips likely provided him with a unique opportunity to spend some extended time with his other family.

Contrasting the experience in Savanna with my mother's Protestant family to that of my dad's parents could not have been any more different. My mom's parents had modest means and utilized their land to grow and harvest much of their food. My dad's parents were in the car business. Prior to the car business, my great-grandfather on the Zimmerman side of the family had been a horse trader in Batavia, IL. My dad's father worked very hard to be in a position to own his dealership; his financial means were very different than my mom's parents.

After my dad's father died in 1976, most of our holidays were spent entertaining my dad's mom, since she was on her own. My mom's parents were loving and kind small-town folk, but my dad's mom, a Jewish Russian immigrant who spent most of her life in the United States, was about as warm and kind as a Russian winter. I know she never really recovered from the loss of my grandfather after his death. On the contrary, my dad's father, William Zimmerman, was super charismatic and warm. My father always spoke lovingly about his dad, how much his father adored my brother and me, and how his father had so looked forward to being a part of our lives growing up. He was an avid sports fan, and my father spoke often of his father's stated desire to take my brother and me to games once we were old enough. I have always felt we were robbed of what should have been many more years of his presence in our lives. Had he not succumbed to cancer when he did, his being around would have made it harder for my dad to disappear as much as he did since my grandfather would have continued running the dealership and my dad would have continued his law practice.

So, when my mother eventually broached the topic with Alan and me, the decision was simple for us: no religion. We didn't want to go to Sunday school—we had heard all about what a pain in the ass it was on Sunday mornings from our friends. After all, we were kids! So that was the end of our religious upbringing. We wouldn't pursue a background in either Christianity or Judaism, and we were just fine with that. Due to our choice, we grew up lacking the typical knowledge about religion that our peers were equipped with. There were benefits, of course, beyond just the free time we gained from religious services. We were fairly unbiased in our feelings about religion in general. I didn't harbor stereotypes that some people did. I heard plenty of inappropriate comments from some of my Catholic friends about Jews—some of them were so ignorant and bigoted.

Yet, I often wonder if the absence of any specific faith disconnected me from the histories interlinked with my own identity. As I spent time around people who came from more serious religious backgrounds, I learned more about how lacking in religion my background was and that my knowledge of the rituals, the symbolism, and the history was shallow at best. I've always deeply felt connected to the inclusiveness of our nation—historically embracing people of all heritages and creeds. However, individually, there are aspects that I feel left out of due to being raised as a hybrid of two religious worlds and having a father who was disconnected from his faith and its traditions.

Looking back on it all, it makes me think of Bill Buckner and that ground ball that went between his legs. Buckner said he leaned on his faith to get him through his mistakes. My father often leaned on his faith as a way to facilitate his mistakes—as a convenient cover for his lies, an alibi for his absence.

CHAPTER 8
MY VISIT WITH MARGARET

A year earlier, I never would've believed that I'd be kicked out of a house by my bigamist dad's second wife.

When my summer on the beach ended in 2013, I just kept on partying through the fall and winter. I was dating multiple women, drinking a lot, seeing ball games, and just living it up as much as I could. I don't think I was aware of how my father's lies and the conflict surrounding them were affecting me. It was just easier to stay busy drinking and hooking up with women than it was for me to face what I was feeling. In retrospect, I think I was terrified to spend any time alone with my thoughts.

What emotional bandwidth I did have was devoted to supporting my mother. I would talk to her every day, sometimes two or three times a day. I was serving as her therapist—talking through what had happened, listening to her thoughts and feelings about it, re-examining past events, and sharing any new information we had learned. It was like piecing together a puzzle—a puzzle of the man we thought we knew so well.

By the summer of 2014, I was back down at the beach, partying. That, my work, and talking to my mother were pretty much my entire life at that point. I didn't realize I was sinking into a deep depression.

I was still dazed and confused about everything that had occurred, and I had been so immersed in the mess that I had not taken a second to process or do any real reflection.

The divorce settlement was to be heard by a judge in Chicago. My brother and I declined to go. We wanted to appear somewhat neutral, although we were obviously on my mother's side. We didn't want to add to the tension or animosity our father was feeling and risk further jeopardizing an already fraught relationship. There was also the consideration of our inheritance, which may sound petty or selfish, but after a lifetime of lies and betrayal, it was all we had left.

There were a lot of things to consider, but ultimately, we thought it was best to just stay out of it. John and Carolyn, however, decided to accompany Margaret and my father to court.

Dad showed up in a wheelchair, still unable to walk following the stroke. He put on quite the show for the judge, attempting to come across as feeble and sick, but the judge wasn't having it. At one point in the proceedings, the judge loudly read a summary of my dad's history, underscoring his misdeeds, and my father had to verbally acknowledge this for the record. "Norman Zimmerman. You married Ann Zimmerman in 1967 and fathered two children with her, Michael and Alan."

My dad squirmed in his chair and mumbled something in agreement.

"Mr. Zimmerman, you have to speak up for the court," the judge ordered.

"Yes, that's correct," he sheepishly replied.

Although I wasn't there, I like to think that at that moment, Margaret and her kids were once again smacked with the truth they had been trying to deny. It was no longer just accusations coming from my mother and me—it was read by a judge in a court of law and confirmed by my father.

I will probably never know what kind of stories, lies, or promises Margaret and my dad fed their kids, but I do know that when I first spoke to Carolyn, I thought I had found an ally. It didn't take long for us to realize that the family had united against us. That was why they showed up at court together that day. It was a statement. Whatever shit was shoveled to win them over, those kids chose to stick by their parents knowing they had lied to them their entire lives. I always found that hard to believe. Granted, when faced with such dramatic details, everyone is going to handle their emotions in different ways, and there is no right or wrong way. However, I would never have accepted being shut up, or paid off to stop seeking the truth. I continued pushing and investigating for years.

The divorce was settled on a Wednesday. I had plans to fly in on Friday and visit my father. On Thursday, Margaret dragged him to the courthouse to get married. One day after the divorce with my mother was settled, she finally got her real, legal marriage. The decades-long sham marriage was finally legal.

Unaware of their new marital bliss, I flew in on Friday as planned, rented a car, and drove right to their house. As I rang the buzzer, I realized I was pretty anxious because I expected Margaret to be there and to answer the door. But to my surprise, it was my father's voice that came over the intercom.

"Hey, Dad, it's Mike," I said into the receiver.

"Oh, Mike," he said reluctantly. "You really shouldn't be here."

"Well, I'm here."

He came to the door in his wheelchair and let me into the foyer. They, of course, had quite a nice house in an upscale neighborhood. I took a seat in the foyer and the two of us chatted for about a half-hour. From where I was sitting, I had a view into the dining room, a partial view into the kitchen, and looking in the opposite direction, I could see the staircase leading to the second floor. The house was well-kept, however, you could tell it had newer-looking furnishings. My parents had always been collectors of fine antiques, and with my mother's design background, our houses were always masterfully designed and decorated. Margaret's house reeked of nouveau riche. I could tell my dad had footed the bill for Margaret to decorate however she wanted, and he probably had little to no input. Nor did he likely care, since he never foresaw the days when he was going to be confined to the premises as he eventually was.

My mother had sent me some of his belongings, which I had dutifully brought for him that day. It was a bunch of papers and assorted items of his that had ended up in a trunk of hers. It included a family photo album we had put together to give him for Christmas back in 2012. He ended up not showing up for Christmas that year, so we hung onto the album to give him at a later time. The album contained photos of all of us dating back to the 70s, capturing us through the years on various trips and at events as a family.

We looked at the album together, looking back on our lives, but I could sense he was very uncomfortable. "You know I can't really keep this here," he told me. He was also concerned that Margaret would come home soon. "She's not going to like this," he said about my visit. "She's down at the hair salon and could be back at any time."

"Well," I suggested. "Why don't you call her and tell her that I'm here and ask her to stay away for a while so we can talk?" In hindsight, it was a pretty dumb idea, but he did exactly that.

"We have company," my dad told her over the phone. "It's Michael."

I severely overestimated her sense of normalcy, as she immediately freaked out. I could hear her on the other end yelling, "*I can't believe you let him in my house!*"

It was yet another miscalculation when it came to dealing with this dysfunctional secret family my father had. It had the opposite effect of what was intended. She came straight home in a fury. She had zero respect for my father's wishes.

Margaret came tearing into the house, ripping mad, and unhinged. She parked her car in the garage and entered the house through the kitchen. I could hear her coming before she was in sight. A hurricane of sound and fury roared through the kitchen and made its way to the foyer where we sat.

"I told you, she's not going to be happy," my father said to me in a matter-of-fact tone.

"*Get out of my fucking house!*" she screamed at me. Turning her rage back to my father, she scolded, "*I can't believe you let him in my fucking house!*" She spewed venom at both of us. Dad didn't react at all—he was probably well used to this kind of behavior and her little fits. I likewise refused to get out of my chair or give her much of a response.

It was not my intention to argue with her or escalate the situation, but I was not done talking with my father. Enraged that I was not listening to her orders, Margaret came over to me and tried to physically pull me out of my chair. She grabbed my left bicep with all her might, dug her nails into my skin, and pulled so hard she left scratches on my arm.

"Look at this," I said to my dad in disbelief, holding my arm up so he could see what she'd done. "Are you going to let her act this way?"

"Mike, I told you she wasn't going to be happy," he said.

Disgusted and incensed, Margaret looked at my father and scoffed. "All you could give me was one day of happiness." From her perspective, she had waited all those years to have an actual, normal, lawful marriage with my father, and one day after she finally got it, I showed up. In her mind, he had betrayed her by letting me into their house. "I'll get my son-in-law over here and he'll kick your ass!" she threatened me.

"I think you should probably go, Mike," my dad said.

That was all I needed to hear. I wasn't going to let her keep me from speaking to my father, but if he wanted me to go, I was going to respect that. "Okay, dad," I said, leaning over to hug him. "I love you."

"I love you too," he said, hugging me back.

This must've crossed Margaret's last nerve because she went absolutely nuclear. She grabbed the pile of stuff I had brought him and flung the front door open so forcefully that it struck the wall, then began chucking all of his belongings out onto the lawn. All this is happening in a community with million-dollar homes, and this woman is out there throwing shit all over their lawn and making a scene like she lived in a trailer park.

"*You get the fuck outta here or I'm calling the police!*" she screamed as I left. She then turned to my father and took another shot at him. "*And I'm sending you away, too!*"

I gathered my dad's belongings off the lawn and left in complete disbelief at what had just happened. I couldn't believe my father had married that nasty, vile, and controlling woman. We had suspected her undue influence in the decisions he made but what I saw that day was beyond what I had imagined. It wasn't just controlling; it was downright abusive behavior.

Back at my hotel room, I got a call from the local police department on my cell phone—the bitch had actually called the cops on me.

"At this time, I have to notify you that you cannot go back to the residence," the officer told me over the phone.

"Look," I said, still in disbelief. "I need to come down there and give a statement because she assaulted me." So, I did exactly that. I showed them my arm and said, "My father let me in the house and she attacked me." They called my father and Margaret but nothing came of it.

"Just don't go back there," an officer told me.

"Do you think I want to go back there?" I asked, incredulously.

When I left the station, I noticed I had a voicemail from my dad: "Mike, you can't come back here. Margaret's going to call the police… She says she's going to send me away…" Part of me couldn't help but think, *well, you made this bed for yourself, dad. Now you gotta lie in it.*

As if all this wasn't enough, I soon got a call from Carolyn acting very much like her mother's daughter. She was irrational, nasty, and accusatory. "Don't you ever go to my mother's house again!" she snapped.

"I was there to see my father. He's my father too," I explained, trying to maintain my composure after a hellish day.

"That's between you and him," she replied dismissively. "You're not allowed at my mother's house."

"The house *my father* paid for?" I asked. "With the money he earned from the car dealership that your family knew nothing about?" She pressed me and I lost my cool. None of this was her fault but she was being such a nasty bitch, so I took it upon myself to remind her of the uncomfortable truth she seemed to be avoiding. "Look," I said. "You're an illegitimate child and your parents lied to you your entire life. If you want to be mad at someone, take it out on them. They're the ones who created the situation we're both in. Don't call me and try to blame me."

She wasn't hearing it. After commanding me to stay away from her mother again, the call ended. The alliance I had imagined with Carolyn was dead. She and Margaret were showing me just how rotten they were.

My mere presence reminded them of the existence of my family, which reminded them of a truth they had chosen to ignore: that they had always been his second family. This filled them with a lot of emotions and they decided to blame me instead of my father.

Shortly thereafter, Margaret followed through on her threats and had my father placed in a nearby nursing home. The purpose of his stay was to do his rehab and get well enough for that hip surgery he still wanted, but I always suspected that it was also her attempt to control him and limit his contact with us. After all, I had heard her threaten to do exactly that.

CHAPTER 9

A FATEFUL TRIP

I t was the summer of 1986, and I was a 15-year-old on the adventure of a lifetime. Unfortunately, it was an adventure that would nearly kill me.

I had the good fortune of being a Boy Scout from an affluent community, which meant our troop had the best equipment and could afford to take extravagant trips. Our Scoutmaster, Thomas Fritts, owned a sporting goods store in Winnetka, so naturally, we were outfitted with the best gear a troop could want. We would frequently take extended camping trips in the Midwest or go canoeing in Arkansas or Tennessee.

However, 1986 marked a special trip. We were going to spend two months hiking and camping across the great state of Alaska. At fifteen, this was a dream for me; eight weeks of scouting in the pristine wilderness of the Great North!

I, along with twenty other scouts and scout leaders, departed in three vans in early June. There were seven of us in our van, and back in those days, the vans had CB radios which we used to communicate with each other on the road. As such, each van needed an identifying handle, and we chose "The Challenger" in memoriam of the seven astronauts who had tragically lost their lives in the space shuttle explosion earlier that year. The name of our van would turn out to be eerily prescient.

The trip itself was fantastic. We saw so much beautiful, untouched wilderness, and hiked the legendary Chilkoot Trail—a significant accomplishment and rite of passage. We camped our way across Alaska, subsisting mostly on freeze-dried camping rations. By late June, we were as far north as Fairbanks, which at that time of the year, saw almost no darkness. One of my most memorable moments was playing softball at 10 pm in broad daylight.

But the highlight of the trip for me was when we hit Anchorage. That's when my father flew in for a ten-day stint with our group. His impeccable timing coincided with salmon fishing on the Kenai River near the town of Soldotna. We spent a couple of days at Fort Richardson Army Base before spending much of the next week fishing the Kenai River. I had been away for over a month at that point, so it was nice to see my dad and spend some quality time with him.

A handful of other dads flew up to join the trip for a week here or there along the way, and it was helpful for the overall morale of the group to see some new faces. I still think back to those vivid memories of being in a boat on the Kenai River with my dad. It was cloudy and cool, and I recall it not feeling like the most relaxing experience. Our guide had the boat moving around a lot in search of better spots to fish the river. But, for me, catching a fish was secondary; I was just happy to be spending time with my dad. After that week when my dad departed, I felt lonely and had to get back into the routine of being on my own. I remember thinking fondly ahead about the next time I would see him. Little did I know what circumstances would accompany our reunion.

On our last night, we sat around the campground in Watson Lake, Yukon Territory, Canada. While there was excitement about the road ahead on our way home, there was also fatigue from roughing it for almost seven grueling weeks in the wilderness.

That evening during dinner, our leaders presented an idea to get us home a few days earlier. I am guessing they could sense the overall fatigue of the group and knew we needed and wanted to get home to our own beds. We all jumped at the idea that we could shave a few days off at the end of the trip. The plan was to wake earlier than normal, and break camp more efficiently to allow for extra time on the road each morning. We would make fewer stops, especially along the more desolate stretches where it wasn't worth stopping. By putting in the extra hours driving each day, we would arrive home two days early.

The next morning, Sunday, August 3rd, we embarked on our race home from the Yukon Territory to Chicago. I vividly recall waking up that morning and immediately breaking camp, then eating breakfast in our vans on the road. We were headed for a midday break at the Laird Hot Springs. Since we awoke very early, we slept in our van that morning. I, along with Jim Rohner and Cam Gilbertson, each slept on one of the three bench seats. John Sexton and David Cullinan slept on the floor of the van beneath us. Our leaders, Jerry Hoynes and Paul Schumann were up front in the captains' chairs driving our van and the cargo trailer attached to it.

At approximately 11:00 AM that morning, as our van began to descend on an unpaved section of the highway, Paul lost control, causing the trailer to jackknife, and sending the van rolling at speeds in excess of 60 mph. The last thing I recall before the accident was briefly waking as we were about to roll. I had not been wearing a seatbelt and was subsequently thrown from the van, landing head-first on the right side of my face. I believe the only thing that saved my life was the fact the road was unpaved, and the earth gave just enough as

I slid on the dirt and gravel road. If that accident had occurred just moments earlier, the road would have been paved, and I would have likely died upon impact.

Cam Gilbertson and Jim Rohner were also thrown from the vehicle. Cam suffered a severed finger, and Jim landed upright, fracturing a vertebra in his back. I was unconscious, bleeding from a severe wound on my face, and would later learn that I had suffered a severe concussion and fractured skull. We were in the middle of nowhere, and while we had standard Boy Scout first aid supplies and strong knowledge of first aid applications, we were dealing with severe injuries that required professional medical attention. As we waited, other travelers eventually came along and were able to get word of our need for help. However, I can only imagine what that wait was like for my uninjured fellow boy scouts. They still had to pick up the pieces from that experience and drive the rest of the way home to Chicago.

After several hours on the side of the road, a neurologist and his family happened upon the scene and he stitched up my face—without anesthesia. I have no recollection of the twenty-six stitches applied to my face. Nor do I have any recollection of the five hours spent on the scene until a helicopter medevacked us to a hospital in Fort Nelson, BC.

My first real memories of the experience were later that evening on August 3rd, while I was still at Fort Nelson Hospital, waiting for an air ambulance to fly me several hours south to Vancouver General Hospital where my injuries would receive the attention they needed. My mom was able to reach the hospital by phone and speak to me. I will always remember that moment; the reassurance in her voice was such a relief, but I was still very much out of it. One vivid memory from the flight down to Vancouver in the air ambulance was my extreme thirst while watching one of the paramedics drink a soda—a strange moment that sticks out in my memory.

Since my accident occurred on a Sunday, my father was not home. It was assumed he was either away fishing or was headed to the office to catch up on paperwork. As we later learned, both were lies. Those were days he would sneak off to his other family. Since my car accident occurred on a Sunday, my mother had the challenge of trying to find my father in an era before cell phones. Eventually, they connected when he called to check in, and since he was supposedly fishing, it was several hours before he returned home. My parents flew out the next day to Vancouver where the World's Fair was underway, making it next to impossible for them to find hotel accommodations. Eventually, they were able to get a room at a nurses' quarters associated with the hospital.

After the first week, I was released from the ICU and spent a night in a room with four other patients, all of us with head injuries. During my entire stay, all I wanted was to sleep, which was no small feat. My head was pounding painfully due to the swelling. Every hour of every night a nurse would walk into the room and drop a bedpan on the floor to ensure everyone was alert. It was a maddening experience. I begged to get out of those circumstances, and during the last few days of my stay, I had a private room and finally got some rest.

When my parents arrived, my mother was warned that I was in bad shape and to brace herself before she walked into the ICU. I do not think she was prepared for what she saw—how could she be? I think I will always recall the moment my parents entered the room. My condition was such that my mother did not recognize me. My face was severely bruised and my eyes were nearly swollen shut. There were twenty-six stitches running across my right cheek and several gashes on my forehead, arms, and legs. I could not walk on my own and required a wheelchair to get around.

After my parents had been visiting me for a while, I asked them to get a mirror for me to see my condition. They hesitantly gave one to me, and my stomach curled when I saw my reflection. I looked like I had gone multiple rounds in the ring with Mike Tyson. Through it all, I suffered multiple skull fractures and a severe concussion. The team of Canadian physicians, who kept me under their care for weeks, eventually released me back into the States. While I was concussed and in severe pain—the IV pumping painkillers into me never felt sufficient—I was aware of my surroundings. It was extremely comforting to see my parents. Nothing else mattered at that point. I wasn't going anywhere fast, and I was resigned to what was going to be a lengthy recovery. I was not discouraged about my long-term prospects for recovery, however. That was likely in part because I was a naïve teen without any true sense of the danger the car accident presented. All that became much more clear to me with time, however, I had a general sense of safety and security with my parents around and being in what seemed to be good medical care.

While I was not showing signs of cognitive disability, I still had a long way to go for a full recovery. When I crossed the border, I looked like a child Frankenstein, with a deep, vertical gash cutting down my cheek. My father, horrified by the deformity, hired one of the top plastic surgeons in the country to make me look normal again. It wasn't until years later, likely during one of my drunken stupors, that the thought occurred to me: My dad's proclivity towards the cosmetic and his willingness to go to great lengths to hide ugly things had benefited me in this circumstance.

I wonder how shaken my parents must have been that day, and I think about how my father had to contend with planning for a sudden ten-day trip to Vancouver with my mom as I healed in the ICU. How did he manage that with Margaret?

My father spent about eight of the ten days in Vancouver before he had to get back to work. I believe the unplanned trip was a challenge for my dad at work, but I suspect the larger challenge for him was managing this unexplained and prolonged absence from his other family. What ensued upon returning home was a lot of fanfare around surviving and the road to recovery. What I recall most though, was the news and gossip that followed.

Back home, I enjoyed a brief stint as a kind of folk hero, the miracle Boy Scout of Winnetka drawing stares, hugs, and handshakes around the small affluent town where I grew up. There was the fallout of the news of my accident hitting Chicago newspapers. My dad undoubtedly had to worry about articles in Chicago papers, mentions on the local evening newscasts, as well as the Pioneer Press Newspapers in the Chicago suburbs. Days after the crash, our community newspaper, the *Winnetka Talk*, published an article under the headline *Scouts Recovering from Yukon Injuries*. The story, splashed across the front page, featured a group photo of Winnetka Boy Scout Troop 20 posed in uniform before our journey from Chicago to Alaska and the Yukon. The piece detailed the near-death collision in northern British Columbia that nearly killed me and three other scouts as our van slid out of control on an Alaskan highway.

It's almost funny now thinking about how that community newspaper article and my newfound celebrityhood posed such a threat to my dad's secret life. He must have been completely unnerved that the life and times of the Zimmermans, which he had worked so hard to keep sealed inside the cocoon of Winnetka, had begun spreading into the surrounding zip codes. He must have worried that my accident would start the unraveling of his hidden world thread by thread.

Once I was home, I underwent plastic surgery to clean the wound on my face. I had routine appointments with neurologists to assess the progress of my healing, ultimately charting a course for how I would navigate my sophomore year in high school. There was concern about headaches, my ability to concentrate, and required absences from all physical activity for the entire school year. I had always enjoyed track but could not resume running again until the following summer, 1987. My dad spent a lot of time shuffling me around to doctor's appointments, but otherwise, we settled back into our routine.

The aftermath of facial surgery turned out to be far more painful than the accident itself. To help lift my spirits upon my release from the hospital, my father treated me to a favorite spoil: a Chicago Cubs game. My face wrapped in bandages, we sat at Wrigley Field behind home plate watching the legendary Nolan Ryan pitch for the Houston Astros. Nolan was past his prime at this point, which was a good thing for Cubs fans. The game was a blast, as we sat surrounded by unruly Cubs fans heckling "Old Man Ryan."

That game is still among my favorite memories with my dad. My love for him became inseparable, intertwined, with my love for the Cubs. The Cubs cemented the bond between my dad and me; they gave us a unique kinship and common language that made me feel special. Anything in life could be expressed to him through our mutual highlight reel of strikeouts, grand slams, and stolen bases at Wrigley.

Looking back, I can see how utterly disruptive it must have been to my father. Surely the news stories were a concern. I also had numerous doctor appointments with neurologists and my dad was heavily involved in the aftermath. John would have been sixteen and Carolyn would have been in junior high. No doubt he needed a very good excuse to give Margaret as to why he was gone for ten days while in Canada. Then he had to find ways to attend several appointments with me.

For me, that whole experience gave me a second chance at life. Carpe diem suddenly wasn't just something I read about in school—it meant a lot to me as a fifteen-year-old, and it went on to shape my outlook and approach to life for a few decades. The event also strengthened my love for my father, who was there for me and spared no resources to help me recover.

I loved my dad. I shared his round face; mop of dark, curly hair; and quick, dry sense of humor. We've always been a lot alike, enjoying a good banter about politics and sports. He taught me how to camp and ski and play hockey. If Alan was a mama's boy, I was definitely a daddy's boy. But by the end of his life, my dad and I had become estranged, driven apart by a near-lifetime of contradictions, paradoxes, lies, and conflicts.

Back then, while recovering from that near-death accident, I was searching for stillness in a maze of pain and turmoil. My head throbbed with the pain as I healed. Stillness came and went, eluding me as it ebbs and flows from our lives.

While reflecting on my trip to Alaska and how that must've affected his ability to maneuver between his two lives, it occurred to me that travel in general was a major disruption to his routine. Despite this inconvenience and risk, my father routinely traveled with my mother and our family. In my discussion with Carolyn, I was not surprised to learn that this was not the case with my father's other family. In fact, he never traveled with them or took them on any real vacations, which makes sense—explaining that kind of prolonged absence to my mother was beyond difficult, whereas Margaret and her family were well-accustomed to such things.

My parents' lengthy travel history can thus be viewed as evidence of my dad's primary loyalties. While he tried to give both families enough time to satisfy them, our family was his first and was prioritized as such.

The following log was assembled by my mother, at my request, to demonstrate exactly that:

> As you know, travel before the car business was limited, as you boys were very young. Norm and I did travel to Washington, DC in November 1972 to visit Neal Ball, who was deputy press secretary for Pres. Nixon. You stayed with your father's parents while we were gone. We, of course, went to Savanna, Illinois often during those years to see my parents. We did go to San Francisco in 1975, and my parents took care of you and Alan while we were away. Norm went into the business in September 1976. We went to Disney World on a business trip in January 1977 and took his mother along. I think we returned to Disneyworld in either 1978 or 1979 with your dad. During these years, there were lots of family trips to Illinois, skiing trips in Northern Michigan, and later Colorado, Utah, etc.
> Automobile business trips began in 1977.

June 1977—Athens, Greece. Side note: I bought a needlepoint rug which is still in my dressing room and a lynx fur coat on that trip.

Sept. 1977—Palm Springs, Cal. Stayed at Canyon Hotel and Racquet Club.

May 1978—Munich and Copenhagen

May 1979—Paris

Recession time between 1980 and 81. Lincoln did not offer trips.

March 1982—Rome and Florence

June 1984—Japan, China, Hong Kong, Hawaii

1986 was the year of your accident in Alaska—Norm was with you. I took Alan on a Caribbean cruise. We were both in Vancouver after your accident.

October 1987—Kona, Hawaii

October 1995—San Francisco Shopping Spree Ritz Carlton

March 1996—Norm and I separated

October 1996—Prague and Munich

July 1997—Venice & Vienna

July 1998—Windstar Cruise Athens to Istanbul

October 1998—Boulders in Scottsdale and Sedona

November 1998—New York Plaza Hotel

July 1998—Sedona to look for property

December 1999—Dana Point for 100 Club followed by 4 days Beverly Hills Shopping Spree

October 1, 2001—I moved to Sedona, Arizona. Norm drove out with me for 2 weeks.

May 2003—GreenBriar

February 2005—Naples 100 Club

CHAPTER 10
UNDUE INFLUENCE

I n late 2014, I flew to Chicago to attend my high school reunion. I decided to visit my father at his rehab facility, but after my last visit, I thought I'd better solicit some help. I contacted one of my father's college buddies, Howard, and asked if he would accompany me on my visit.

Howard had been a friend of dad's and our whole family for decades. Howard and my dad attend the University of Illinois and Northwestern Law School together—a relationship that went back almost 60 years. He and his wife had been close with my mother and father my entire life. They had kids who were around the same age as my brother and me, and we would get together with them often. My father was quite fond of Howard. I figured having him with me would be disarming if Margaret was there or found out about my visit.

When the truth came out, Howard had been in disbelief about the whole thing. His wife, however, had remarked at one point during a conversation with my mother that she wasn't surprised. "I always thought something was off with him," she said. For sixty years, she had harbored this feeling that my father wasn't being genuine.

I don't think Howard had any real interest in visiting my father. Everyone who found out the truth was quite repelled by it. No one wanted to support him, but Howard was a friend to the family, and as a favor to me, he agreed to come with me to the rehab facility.

We met outside in the parking lot at the Westmoreland rehab facility, which is part of Northwestern Hospital in Lake Forest, and headed towards my father's room. The floor on which my father was staying felt like the typical nursing home/rehab facility I had seen before. It was quiet. There were a few elderly people in wheelchairs, and the nurses did not seem to care we were there. There was an industrial sterileness to the setting. On the door to his room was a handwritten note: NO VISITORS. Margaret was trying to keep him isolated. We knocked on the door and entered. My father had just woken up from a nap and was fairly amicable about our presence. He was surprised we were there but still very receptive.

He called for a nurse, who helped him into his wheelchair, and the three of us went out to visit in the lounge area. We sat and shot the shit for a bit, talking about sports and safe, non-confrontational topics. Howard stuck around for about a half hour or so before leaving. At that point, my father and I continued to chat, steering clear of conversation that would lead to conflict. When Margaret did come up, I couldn't help but ask, "Why does she act that way?"

"You know, Mike, I can't explain it… It's just one of those things, " he said.

That was the general dismissal I would get whenever anything related to Margaret and his other family would come up. His defenses were up. After the fallout with Carolyn, he wasn't going to tell me anything. He was trying to keep things close to the chest.

I didn't push—it had been a relatively nice visit, and I didn't want to cause any tension or animosity.

On Sunday, I went back to watch the Bears game with him. It was nice to hang out with him and pretend that everything was okay. We talked about football, my brother, my mother, and my career, but we steered clear of the elephant in the room. Everything was fine except for the fact that I could see he was nervous that Margaret or one of their kids might show up. He was noticeably uneasy.

I left feeling very uncomfortable about his situation. I remembered Margaret telling my father she was going to send him away, then seeing the note on his door. I knew she didn't want him to see us, but I began to wonder just how much control she had over him. He seemed genuinely afraid of her finding out I was there. I had mixed emotions about what appeared to be Margaret's mistreatment of my dad. He was my dad, and it was all still so fresh, despite being almost 18 months into the situation at that point. On the one hand, I felt protective of him and thought Margaret was being abusive, and much of that feeling resided in the fact that I missed my dad. I missed the dad I knew before mid-June 2013. On the other hand, there was a part of me that felt he deserved it. How do I reconcile those emotions? Did he deserve any empathy from me? Those questions troubled me for a long time. Eventually, as I sank deeper toward rock bottom, I arrived at those answers for myself.

From there, I went straight to the airport and flew back home to Philly. It was the last decent face-to-face interaction I had with my father. At the time, I did not realize that would be the case. I was not naïve about what the future had in store for my father and me. I was realistic about the impact of what learning about his double life meant to me. I had no false illusions of our relationship ever being restored. At the time in late 2014, all the details were still sinking in. Forty-plus years of my life and my entire relationship with my father had been turned on their head in just 18 months. I had no idea how much worse it was all going to get. Yet, it did get worse—much worse.

A few months later, in February 2015, I was on a business trip to North Carolina when I spoke to him on the phone and found out he was ill. He believed he had pneumonia and told me he was being admitted to the hospital for observation. He seemed confused, maybe a little scared about his condition, but he remained mostly positive.

A couple of days later, I called his room to check on him and Margaret answered. "Who's this?" she demanded to know.

"It's Michael," I said, calmly.

She turned the phone over to my dad, who said, "Mike, you really shouldn't call here."

In the background, I could hear her telling him, "Tell him *not* to call here anymore. He isn't allowed to call you!" She was always yelling background commentary when I spoke to him on the phone. Once, when he and I were talking about my mother's breast cancer, Margaret was in the background yelling, "I hope she fucking dies!"

Her refusal to let me speak with him didn't sit right with me at all. She was keeping him from his family. She was controlling who had access to him, screening his calls, and controlling what he said to others. He acted terrified of her and was completely different toward me when she was not around. She had previously threatened to "send him away" and had then proceeded to move him to several new facilities, seemingly changing locations whenever we found him. Through our conversations with these various rehab centers and the hospital, we were able to conclude that Margaret had power of attorney over him.

We began to suspect that she was exerting undue influence over him and that his ability to exercise control over his life had been compromised. Based on my last conversation with him, I wasn't even sure if he was competent any longer. Despite everything he had put us through, we were concerned for him. So, in the spring of 2015, we sued for guardianship.

Dad was livid. He now had to spend money on attorneys to essentially defend Margaret. From there, things escalated quickly. Our attorneys successfully argued that we should have access to my father's estate plan, which made Margaret very angry. We were also able to get the court to appoint a guardian ad litem, who would interview all parties involved and determine if any undue influence was being exerted on my father.

The guardian ad litem process was frustrating. I have no idea how thorough or unbiased it was. My conversations with the guardian were long-distance, and his appointments with my father were pre-arranged. Margaret always had notice of when he was coming. I found this to be absurd. "You have to show up and catch them off-guard if you want to get an honest assessment," I urged him. But that was not how the process was done.

In the end, my father was found competent and the court refused to assign a guardian to take over the power of attorney from Margaret. All this incited more anger and resentment from my father.

"You sued me, Mike!" he charged.

"No," I said. "You're an attorney; you know how all of this works. If the roles were reversed, and this was happening to your father, you'd be fighting it, too."

He refused to admit that or concede any of my points. In his eyes, this was a betrayal. He remained bitter and angry over a situation his lies and actions had caused. It was easier to blame us, and this soured our relationship. I have no regrets about pursuing the guardianship case. It was the only way to somewhat level the playing field and get straight answers on where my brother and I stood. Not to mention if there was undue influence and abuse, as it appeared, then I wanted it dealt with through the proper legal channels.

When we finally got access to his estate planning, we found out that my brother and I had been removed from the plan. He had cut us out right after marrying Margaret. During the divorce, we discovered that my father had various life insurance policies. One of the policies that were sizeable and had reasonable premiums had Carolyn and John as beneficiaries. As part of the divorce settlement, that plan had to be changed to include my brother and me, and my half-siblings were taken out. I suspect that to get them to sign off on that, he agreed to take us out of the estate plan. Now the plan said that everything was to go to Margaret, which is exactly what happened when he died in 2020.

We got completely screwed out of everything.

My grandfather had set up some trusts that were supposed to go to my brother and me, but my father was the trustee, which left him with a lot of discretion as to how the funds could be utilized. As we look back on the entire transition that occurred between my grandfather and my uncle, Paul, when my uncle left the car business, we can see how the role my father played in stealing the car store from his brother. Paul was supposed to take over the business, however, when Paul started to push for more ownership, and to move my grandfather closer to retirement, my father, acting as my grandfather's attorney, pounced. He was able to get Paul bought out, leaving my aging grandfather alone in running the store. My father saw the opportunity to get his hands on the golden goose, which he badly needed to support two families. At the time we got to see the estate plans, he had not designated beneficiaries on the trusts my grandfather had established, thus leaving it to his estate. Not only had our memories and relationships been lies—everything that was promised to us for two generations amounted to nothing more than just another lie in the end.

To this day, we have no idea what was left when he died or how much Margaret got. It could've been millions, or it could've been nothing. He may have been living off it and spent most of it. Those rehab centers weren't cheap. But not knowing hurts; it's a reminder of how we were cut out and deprioritized without a second thought. It is details like these that solidify what a sociopath my father truly was. The ability to show so little emotion towards us, shifting gears to do what suited his circumstances best to ensure he was taken care of by Margaret for the last seven years of his life with little regard for the impact it had on my brother and I, speaks volumes about my father's character.

My father would say that he had taken care of us during his life. I guess that's a fair point, but he never should've had a second family to begin with. That meant he paid for their health insurance, college tuition, and everything else. A whole lifetime of expenses from another family. It's also hard not to think about how he chose to preserve this lie and live that lifestyle, and how it limited his success with the car dealership. His dealership was located on a strip that had a bunch of other dealerships. Those dealerships all turned over ownership at one point or another during his tenure. He could've been buying those up and building a real legacy. The obvious move would've been to do exactly that, then have my brother and I run our own dealerships—but he didn't want that. He couldn't afford to have us involved with the business because that would've been risky. It would've been too easy for the truth to get out. It's also because by owning just one dealership, he was able to keep a low profile. If he owned seven or eight, Margaret and her family might have figured it out.

The guardianship fight was unsuccessful in accomplishing much other than hardening my father's resentment toward us. The only solace was that we were able to access the estate plan, but that too was more of a blow to us than it was a victory. There was this finality to it as if dad had divorced not just mom but his own sons too. Though, I suppose it was better to find out then than it would've been after his death.

I was exhausted by the whole ordeal at this point. The lies, the drama, the lawyers, the unreasonable and entitled second family—it was wearing on me mentally and emotionally. Following the guardianship battle, my father was angry, and I was hurt. After the events of 2015, I wouldn't see him again for four years.

CHAPTER 11
MY FATHER'S LAST CHANCE

Throughout the whole ordeal, I tried to keep some channels open with my father. My attorneys advised me to keep engaging with him, and as much as I was hurt, I still carried some hope that we could have some sort of a relationship moving forward. Sure, I was angry as hell at him, but he was still my father. As such, I sent him birthday cards and would occasionally call and leave messages. Since it seemed there was undue influence by Margaret, despite what the guardian ad litem had determined, my attorneys felt there was potential to challenge the estate upon my father's death. They felt it was important to continue to maintain a relationship with my father especially as it pertained to challenging my father's use of the trusts my grandfather had established to benefit my brother and me.

My brother Alan did so as well but in a much more confrontational, antagonistic way. While I was trying to keep the peace and keep things amicable, my brother could not resist poking our father in the eye whenever he had the chance. He would make sarcastic or accusatory comments about our father, his character, or his other family, like: "I can't believe you're choosing to have a relationship with your illegitimate children over us." He'd always had a more distant relationship with our father, who was never really there for him the way he was for me. Now my brother realized that dad was never around because he was spending time with his other family, and he carried a lot of resentment about that. (Rightfully so.) My brother had every right to feel the way he did about what my dad did to him. He needed my dad's presence in his life more than my dad actually was, and my brother's progress during his pre-teen and teen years suffered as a result. I do not agree with my brother's approach to how he vented his anger about the situation once we found out about the double life and secret family my father had. However, he is entitled to his feelings about such an impactful set of circumstances.

In September 2015, I decided to make one last trip to see my father. I wasn't looking for a fight or to throw anything in his face. At this point, I just wanted answers so I could perhaps begin to find some closure and move on. I thought that maybe now, after everything had cooled off, he might be willing to at least give me the answers I wanted. What difference would it make now? Telling me the truth would not affect his situation.

"You should come, too," I urged Alan. "This could be the last time you get to talk to dad. Come with me, and we can do this together. It's your opportunity to confront him in person."

"Absolutely not," he told me. He wanted no part of it.

"I understand," I said. "But I'm going to go. If there's anything you want to say to him, put it in a letter and I will bring it to him."

There was a lot of anger in my brother's letter. It was full of incendiary barbs and remarks about my father's behavior, and it left me in a tough place. I certainly didn't begrudge my brother for feeling the way he did, but I knew that the things he said were not going to help or be productive in any way. So, I took a black marker and redacted some lines, then made a photocopy of the letter to bring with me.

If my father looked at it, he would know why I had covered parts of it—but it was still less inflammatory than seeing the scathing words my brother had scrawled.

I arrived in Chicago around 11:30 am and headed to my dad's rehab facility. He was surprised to see me. "Mike, what are you doing here?" He was noticeably colder than usual.

"I'm here to see you. I wanted to come talk to you."

We chatted for a bit before I asked him, "Dad, do you care that this might be the last time you see me?"

"Yeah, I do," he said.

"So, tell me how all this happened. Tell me the truth about it all."

He waved his hand dismissively. "Not this again."

"Take me back to the late 60s. I know you were a young attorney. I can't believe you planned all of this. Who would want to be stuck between two lives?"

"Oh, you know, Mike. It's been so long," he muttered. "My memory isn't what it used to be. I have a hard time concentrating since the stroke, you know. I have a hard time even reading the paper."

What utter bullshit. He was with it enough to convince the guardian ad litem that he was competent. His mental lapses only seemed to occur when it came to discussing his deceit. "I'm asking you, as your son, who you might not ever see again, to tell me your side of the story. Explain to me how all this happened. I'm giving you a chance to tell me straight."

"It just happened, Mike. I ended up with Margaret, and she's a wonderful woman."

"C'mon, dad. Tell me the truth."

He looked away and shook his head. "You'll just tell the other kids."

After all that, he was still afraid that they would find out more. He must've known that he had given them a raw deal throughout their lives. He essentially cheated them, and he didn't want them to know the full extent of it.

"Dad, I'm just looking for answers for myself. For my peace of mind. I have no desire to throw anything in Carolyn's or John's face."

He couldn't bring himself to tell me, unfortunately. It was the last in a long series of disappointments from him. We talked a little more about my mother and my brother and my life, but it was all a bit stiff and uncomfortable; I imagine there was a degree of humiliation he felt. He had been my best friend and I had looked up to him. Now he had to face the fact that his biggest fan knew he was a fraud, a liar, an adulterer, and a bigamist by most standards. I think that deep down, he was embarrassed.

I pressed him on what Margaret had known or thought she was all these years. All he said was, "I just kind of think of it like a common law situation." To me, that means they both knew they weren't legally married before 2014.

I'm still amazed he somehow made it all work. My father was a sociopathic manipulator who needed a different approach to handling each of his women. My mother was bright and independent and was quite alright with him not being around all the time, but Margaret was a different story. She never stuck me as particularly bright, and he fed her a ton of lies. She never even knew about the dealership. She knew she was a kept woman.

I read what was left of Alan's letter to him, and he told me that he wanted to keep it. So, I put it up on the top shelf of his closet in a little cabinet they had for him. It was too high for him to reach. I also propped it up so that when Margaret came by, she would see it and know I had been there. They had tried so hard to keep him isolated from us. I just wanted to subtly let her know that it hadn't worked and that I had indeed been by to visit.

The nurses came to check on him, and I asked one to take a picture of us. It was partly because my mother had been inquiring about his condition, but also because part of me knew it was the last time I would see him. He had never gotten over the guardianship fight and was never the same with me. There may have been other lies he was protecting with his silence—things he either didn't want me and Alan to know, or things he didn't want Margaret, Carolyn, and John to know. Maybe both. He likely viewed me as a liability or even a threat to some of his existing lies. Sharing details with me to give us clarity would just increase the risk of the other family finding out, too.

Or his bitterness had hardened and he just didn't give a damn about us anymore. "You're probably not going to see me again," I told him. He didn't care. We were already dead to him. He'd made peace with that and chosen the other family to live out his dying days with.

I had realistic expectations that day. I wasn't expecting him to tell me anything or to plead for me to remain in his life— yet I was still disappointed. I think what hurts the most is that he wasn't willing to be straight with me. I knew he hadn't purposely gotten tied up with two women and decided to have children with both of them within 14 months of each other. Nobody plans that. He got himself into a situation and got stuck. A big part of me just wanted to hear him admit that—I wanted him to prove he was still a decent person on some level and still cared for me, even if he had made some serious mistakes. But in the end, what I thought and felt just didn't matter to him at all.

After a lifetime of lies and then screwing us out of our inheritance, this was the one thing he could've done—the *least* he could've done—to give me some closure. But he simply refused. That cemented for me the fact that I did not know this man. He was an enigma. The man I thought I had known did not exist. I had been so close to him but I didn't know him at all. That's alarming and unsettling. Think about investing so much of yourself in your role model, your father, to then find out decades later that he was far from the person you were led to believe all that time. It is truly astonishing and heartbreaking.

That was the last time I spoke with my father. I believe Margaret found my brother's letter and knew I had visited. All subsequent phone calls to the nursing home switchboard requesting a transfer to his room were denied. I was told that under the direction of Margaret, no calls were to be connected—yet another example of Margaret denying us access to our father.

Eventually, my brother's behavior, with his inappropriate comments, provoked a response as well. In the summer of 2016, after receiving Father's Day cards from us, my father got an attorney to instruct us to cease all contact and warned us that any further attempts to contact him could result in legal action. Again, it was easier to lash out at us than it was to face the shame of what he had done and how it was affecting us. It may have been my father taking action, however, I know from his past comments to me how angry Margaret got when we sent him cards to their house. What a wonderful woman Margaret is.

CHAPTER 12

HIS FINAL YEARS

Near the end of 2015, my father finally had his hip surgery and was able to leave the rehab facility. At this point, he was isolated from us. We'd managed to hunt him down every time Margaret had moved him to a new facility, but now that he was home with her, it became impossible to speak with him. For nearly three years, we had almost no idea what he was up to or how he was. That changed in August 2018 when my cousin Diane visited him at his home.

Diane was one of two children of my father's brother, Paul. Diane had lived in the Chicago area most of her life except for the prior 15 years or so when she lived in Colorado and Utah. My father had often helped her and her husband financially. Diane had been very helpful with my grandmother while she was alive, and I think my father always remembered that. I also suspect my father had some guilt about cutting his brother out of the car business. So, when Diane or her husband needed a car, my dad would cut them a deal at the dealership. He'd even occasionally send them cash.

In the summer of 2018, Diane contacted me to tell me she was thinking of reaching out and contacting my father when she was visiting Chicago. At this point, our whole family was wondering how he was doing and what his health was like. "Feel free to call," I told her. "But I don't know if you'll get a response." I had major doubts that Margaret would allow her to access my father. To my surprise, when Diane called, she spoke to Margaret, and Margaret let her speak with Dad. The two chatted for a while and Diane floated the idea of coming by for a visit. There was a little back and forth, but at some point, Dad agreed.

So, Diane went to their house. Margaret let her in and led her through the living room to an office that they'd converted into my dad's bedroom; his immobility prevented him from climbing the stairs. They'd rented a hospital bed from a medical supplier for the room, and that was pretty much where he stayed. He needed help to even get out of bed, which was too much for Margaret to handle. Instead, John or Carolyn's husband, Mark, would help. If neither of them was around, the medical aides they had coming to the house every day would assist him. The man who had used his constant mobility to facilitate his lies and balance his time between his two families was now stuck in his bed, dependent on others for every facet of his life. There's something poetically karmic about that. He quite literally had to lie in the bed he had made for himself.

According to Diane, he was pretty much cut off from the world. He had no phone, no cell phone, no access to the internet, or anything like that. There wasn't even a TV in the room. I can't help but wonder if Margaret was punishing him. They had a lot of money and resources and lived in a nice house. It's hard to believe they couldn't have made things a little more comfortable for him.

"This is my life right now," he told her, gesturing to the room.

In preparation for her visit, I peppered Diane with some questions for her to ask about his health and circumstances. But from all indications, it seems she didn't have to pry. Dad was forthcoming about his situation and she was able to ascertain things about his health just by observing how he was living. My father had a lot of questions for her, so they talked for a while about her, her husband, and everything that was going on in her life.

He did ask about me, my brother, and my mother—as if behind all the lies and the detached façade, somewhere deep inside, he still cared for us. At least, as much as he was capable of caring for others. I still don't know how much he cared, nor if his disregard for us was rooted in ambivalence or shame. I suspect there was a little of both. I didn't necessarily expect us to come up during Diane's visit, but I thought it was a possibility, and I had provided her with our phone numbers to give to him if the opportunity allowed. She gave him the numbers, which he took, only to mention that he wasn't sure he would be able to get to a phone. He was essentially a captive in his own home; Margaret made the rules.

All in all, I am fascinated and a little baffled as to why Margaret let her visit him. I have to assume that she viewed Diane as a non-threatening member of his family—someone he had supported and had a relationship with for a long time. It wasn't just some random person showing up whom Margaret had never heard of. So, for whatever reason, Margaret decided that Diane was safe, but my brother and I were not. I guess Diane was low-risk; she wasn't going to run off and have conversations with Margaret's children. There's also the distinct possibility that Margaret knew we would find out Diane had visited, and this was her way of giving us a nice, "Fuck you" from afar.

Knowing that his health wasn't great and that he might not be around for much longer, I decided to try and visit him one last time. I was traveling to Chicago again for another high school reunion and figured I would give it a shot. My life was changing for the better at this point: I was going to be a father, and despite everything that had happened, I wanted to share that news with my dad. I decided it was best to recruit another of Dad's old friends to accompany me, so I reached out to one of them, a guy named Harvey.

Harvey had been friends with my dad dating back to college. They'd been good friends for decades. Harvey worked for the Chicago Blackhawks in various roles for a long time. He would often give us tickets to games, and knew all of us well. So, when I called and told him I wanted to go visit my father, he was already well aware of the situation and gladly agreed to come along.

I flew in, rented a car, and met Harvey at a mall near my father and Margaret's house. On the way to their house, we tried to figure out a game plan. "I'm wondering what we're going to say over the intercom when Margaret answers," I said.

"You think she'll answer?" Harvey asked.

"Probably. It's like he's in hiding in there."

"Right," said Harvey, mulling options. "So, what should we say? I'm assuming if we told her it's Mike and Harvey, she won't let us see him."

I nodded. "And you wouldn't just show up out of the blue," I added. "So, you can't just tell her it's you."

"We just need to get him to the door," said Harvey.

"Maybe we just tell her we have a delivery for Norman."

Harvey nodded. "Seems harmless enough. Should work, right?"

Our plans set, we arrived at the house. We walked up, climbed the front stoop, and rang the bell. A couple of minutes passed and nothing happened. "Let's try going around," I suggested. "His bedroom is on the side of the house." I figured perhaps Margaret was not home and he was unable to answer the door.

We walked around to the right side of the house and approached my dad's bedroom window. We could see through the cracks of the blinds and saw my father lying in his bed. A medical aide was also in the room with him. So, we knocked on the window and identified ourselves, but there was no reaction of any kind.

Not five minutes later, we saw a police car pull up. Harvey and I walked back around front and met the officer in the driveway. The officer was fairly courteous—I'm sure it helped that I had an 80-year-old man with me. We didn't exactly look like prowlers or anything. Margaret had threatened to call the cops if I ever showed up again, but it had been five years since then. I didn't think just ringing their doorbell would prompt her to call the police, but she did, and they showed up very quickly. She was probably waiting for the day that I tried again. She was that petty.

"What's going on, gentlemen?" the officer asked as he emerged from his car.

"Hi, I'm Michael Zimmerman. My father, Norm, lives here. This is his friend of sixty years, Harvey. We're just here to visit him."

"Oh, okay," the officer replied. "Wait here," he said before heading to the front door. There's a fairly long sidewalk that leads from the driveway to the front door, so we were out of view. We wanted to comply with the officer's directions, so we just waited for him to come back. "He and his wife are not interested in seeing you guys," the officer informed us upon his return. "I'm sorry, but you'll have to go."

I dug into my pocket and pulled out a picture of an ultrasound. "Look, I know Margaret isn't a fan of mine, but I'm not here to cause trouble. I wanted to tell my father that he's going to be a grandfather. That's all."

The officer looked at the ultrasound photo and nodded. "Okay, I understand," the officer replied. "Hold on one sec." He went back to the front door and explained the situation to no avail. "I'm sorry, but he said he doesn't want to see you guys," the officer told us when he came back.

"Okay," I said, disappointed. "What about just Harvey?" I asked.

"No," the officer reiterated. "I'm sorry, but he doesn't wish to see either of you."

"Okay, I understand," I said. "We'll leave."

As we drove away, I had a lot of emotions. I felt angry, resentful, and hurt. I was disappointed that the man I once considered my best friend didn't want to share this moment with me—didn't want to know about my son. But I was also spiteful and took some solace in the fact that I knew our visit had royally pissed off Margaret. I thought about her going crazy over it, bitching and moaning, wondering how I dared to show up at her home. If nothing else, at least we'd ruined her day.

I didn't attempt to contact him again after that, nor did I hear anything else about him until May 2020 when my mother called. "Your father died."

"Really?" I asked. "How did you find out?"

"I got a letter," she explained, "from Social Security, informing me that my payments are going to increase because Norman had passed away."

There was a stunned silence. It was not such a shock that he had died, but it was hard to believe that we had to find out through a letter from Social Security. We had no idea when he had died or how because we figured Social Security probably takes time to process things. So, I went online to the Lake County, IL website and found a place where, after providing some proof of my identity, I was able to order a death certificate. I expected it to take some time, but to my surprise, it showed up at my door just two days later.

My father passed away on April 21st, after being hospitalized with COVID-19 for 10 days. COVID had ravaged his body, leaving him with bacterial pneumonia and several other fatal conditions. My father had become one of the victims of the terrible pandemic. In a tragic twist of irony, he had caught COVID from one of the medical aides that were coming to the house to take care of him. Margaret had caught it too but was able to weather it, unlike my father, whose health was already compromised.

I think about Dad's final days a lot—how he was mostly isolated from the world, only seeing the people who were there to wipe his ass and help him into his wheelchair, and how one of those people gave him COVID. From there, due to his health, he was quickly hospitalized. Due to the protocols at the time, nobody was able to visit him. COVID was still relatively new, so I doubt they understood that when he went into the hospital, the odds of him coming home were never good. My father suffered for almost two weeks and died alone. The man with two families had nobody by his side in the end. I can't help but consider karma when I think about it. I have mixed feelings, but it's the end he chose through his actions.

We all thought this would mark the end of the drama, but we were wrong. A couple of weeks after hearing of my father's death, my mother received a phone call from Social Security. They wanted certificates, dates of divorce, and any other documentation my mother had regarding her and my dad's relationship. The office told my mom someone was challenging the Social Security benefit. We suspect Margaret was challenging the benefits my mother had been awarded. Even though Margaret was legally married to my father at the time of his death, it had only been since 2014; the rest of their marriage had been a farce. Social Security had informed Margaret that to receive extra benefits from my father's passing, they would've had to have been married for ten years or more. I don't know if it was ignorance, pride, or spite, but for whatever reason, Margaret decided to challenge this—all over less than a couple grand a month. She wanted that money to go to her, not my mother. After everything she'd already gotten and the inheritance she and her family had screwed us out of, she still wasn't satisfied.

I wonder if she felt my father owed it to her. I remember him saying to me during one of our last visits, "You know, Mike, neither woman has been very happy with me." My father promised Margaret things—a life together, that she would be taken care of. In the end, she probably felt she'd been screwed over too.

There's also the distinct possibility that my father had spent the majority of his wealth in his final years. The rehab facilities and at-home medical aides were not cheap. It is possible that when all was said and done, Margaret didn't have much left. To her, that extra little bit of Social Security money might have made the difference. I'll probably never know, but regardless, the benefits were not hers to claim. She lost the challenge, and there was no change to my mother's Social Security benefit.

That was the last we heard from Margaret. Our strangely interwoven lives had untangled themselves with my father's death. She got a multimillion-dollar house and whatever inheritance and life insurance money there was; we got a bunch of shitty memories.

During the course of their conversations back in 2014, Margaret had mentioned to Patty that there would not be an obituary when my father eventually passed away. It's easy to imagine why she wouldn't one, but we made sure there was one. To honor my father, and in a final act of defiance to Margaret and her kids, I placed an obituary in all the Chicago papers:

> *Norman Zimmerman, long-time Chicago and Winnetka resident, died April 21st. Norman was born in Chicago in 1936. After graduating Roosevelt High School, he attended U of Illinois and later graduated from Northwestern Law School. He practiced law many years before entering the family business, Schaumburg Lincoln Mercury 1976-2012. He is preceded in death by parents, William B. and Ann Sacharin Zimmerman, his brother Paul, his niece Diane Zimmerman Johnston. He is survived by son Michael(Beth), Malvern, PA.; son Alan, Scottsdale, AZ: and his ex-wife Ann C. Zimmerman, Scottsdale, AZ. His present wife whom he married in 2014, and two children. Services have been held.*

A nice photo of my dad ran with the obits. I ran it in as many papers as I could think, and also asked a friend of mine to clip the obituary and mail it to Margaret. I am confident Margaret and her family saw it.

It was a fitting tribute to my father and a final middle finger to Margaret. I was his legitimate son, and I got to have a say on the final record of his life. The obituary made clear that we were his initial, legal, and primary family. I'm sure that pissed her off. It was a tiny morsel of satisfaction that I got at the end of everything. She had kept my father away from us and advanced a lie to her children and who knows how many others, but in the end, she couldn't rewrite the truth. In his death, those things she had wanted to bury and deny were indelibly recorded for public record. In the end, the record showed where they had stood all along.

These photos span over forty-five years showing how involved and very much a part of our lives my father was throughout that entire time. There were no breaks or gaps in his involvement during those years, as he was actively a part of our lives as a family. The photos serve to help illustrate why uncovering his secret double life was so traumatizing for me.

December 1967: Dad and Mom, wedding photo.

1971: Dad and me.

1971: Mom, Dad, and me.

1972: Dad, his mother, his grandmother, and me.

1972: Dad and me.

1972: My parents in Vegas with the Kattens.

July 1975: Dad, Alan, and me. 4th of July in Winnetka.

Fall 1978: Mom, Dad, Alan, and me.

1979: Dad, Alan and me (in Cubs hat) in the backyard of our house on Ash Street in Winnetka.

Early 80s: Dad in the car business.

Christmas 1980: Dad, Alan, and me.

1983: Dad, Alan, and me on a ski trip in Upper Michigan.

1984: Dad, Alan, and me at Mackinac Island.

1984: Mom and Dad in Paris, on a trip with Ford Motor Company.

1985: Dad, Alan, and me fishing in Mountain Home, Arkansas.

1985: My parents.

Spring 1989: Dad, Alan, and me in London.

*June 1989: Me with my parents at my graduation
from New Trier High School.*

1989: Dad, Alan, and me at The Louvre.

1991: Alan, Dad, and me in Lake Tahoe.

March 1991: Article from Pioneer Press *in Winnetka. My parents in photo.*

May 1993: Dad and me at my graduation from University of Rochester.

1994: My parents at the ceremony where my mom was named Winnetka Woman of The Year.

1996: Dad and Alan at his graduation from University of Iowa.

Christmas 1999: Mom, Dad, Alan, and me.

2001: Dad and me in Chicago.

2003: Alan, Dad, and me at Wrigley Field.

2003: Dad and me at the Grand Canyon.

Christmas 2005: My dad, Alan, and me, near Sedona.

Christmas 2009: Mom, Dad, Alan, and me in Sedona.

October 2010: Dad and Mom.

Christmas 2011: Alan, Dad, and me in Scottsdale.

*Father's Day Weekend 2012: Dad and me at Wrigley Field
for what ended up being our last Cubs game together.*

*September 2015: Visiting dad when he was staying at
Whitehall Assisted Living Facility in Deerfield, IL.*

CHAPTER 13

HINDSIGHT

E very family has a shared experience that binds them together. It's their memories of those experiences that help ensure the strength of those bonds as the years go by. For my family, that has been taken from us. The shared experience of our life together has been revealed to have been built on a foundation of lies. The hardest part of processing and moving on from that are how my father's deceptions left me with a lifetime of tainted memories. Recollections of love and joy and fondness still surface, as they would for anyone, but in my mind, they quickly turn sour. There's this feeling that they can't be trusted—that the feelings I recall in these moments are themselves full of untruths and contradictions.

As my family and I look back, we've been able to piece together a lot of what we didn't know at the time. Certain red flags stand out now—events that didn't make sense at the time, but that were never given much scrutiny.

One of the earliest red flags was after I was born. For the first two years of my life, we lived in Chicago, near Wrigley Field. My mother wanted out of the city before I started preschool, but Dad objected and made a fuss about not wanting to leave the city. The real reason for his hesitance was that he already had Margaret stashed in the suburb of Morton Grove, and he didn't want his two worlds to collide. Eventually, Mom got her way, and my father agreed to move to Winnetka. And so began our suburban lives, which were also full of red flags concerning my father's behavior.

The holidays were a time when many of those red flags would go up. Every Thanksgiving morning, my father would wake up early and head out. His excuse was that he was going to collect rent at one of the apartment buildings he owned. It was a routine he kept every year—one which my mother probably begrudgingly accepted. My brother and I certainly didn't think anything of it. When you're a kid, your parents set the course, and you're just along for the ride.

In hindsight, it's an absurd story. Pounding on doors to collect rent on Thanksgiving is almost cartoonish—was he Ebenezer Scrooge? Who goes to collect rent on Thanksgiving? Thanksgiving doesn't even fall at the beginning of the month; rent wasn't due. And these apartments weren't in the best part of town. My father was tough, but he wasn't *that* tough. I don't think he'd actually have gone knocking on doors, interrupting people's family time on a holiday, to demand rent. He and Jimmy Adelman did own an apartment building in the early 70s—that part was true. However, they had gone separate ways and sold that building. My father claimed he still owned one; that was a lie. He was spending Thanksgiving day with his other family before coming to us in the late afternoon and evening. Eventually, after his mother died, and he had claimed he no longer owned the apartment building, he used the excuse of visiting his parents' gravesite on Thanksgiving. He knew that was ironclad—after all, what was my mom going to say to him about visiting his parents' grave?

But that was a typical day for us. Dad would be up and gone early, and mom would spend her entire day scrambling to get the food ready. My cousin Diane would often come for dinner with her husband, and, while she was still alive, my father's mother would join us as well. Diane would typically pick up my grandma and bring her to the house around 4 or 5 PM. The idea was that we would have dinner at 6. Of course, my father was always late for everything. But sometime after 6, he would stroll in and we would all eat.

Well, when I was sharing details with Carolyn, we discovered we had been sharing our father on Thanksgiving. Dad would get up early and head over to Margaret's place, where they would have dinner at 1 PM. He would then peddle some excuse to them and leave in time to come home and eat a second dinner with us. Who eats two Thanksgiving dinners? I guess that's why ours was so late in the day—my father needed time to eat with his other family and then digest enough to have room for meal number two.

Christmas was another holiday my father managed to split between his two families without either knowing any better.

Starting back when they were dating, my father had set the expectation with my mother that on Friday nights he would always go out and play cards with his friends. My father was Jewish, so he used that as an excuse to cut out on some of our Christmas traditions. Every year in our neighborhood, one family would host a Christmas Eve party. We would always go as a family, but by 6 or 7 o'clock, he was gone. It was his tradition, he maintained, to go play cards with a bunch of his fellow Jewish attorneys. He would take off and come home very late, around 2 or 3 in the morning. Then he would be there on Christmas morning with us and we'd spend Christmas together. But he was never around on Christmas Eve.

Come to find out, Christmas Eve was reserved for spending time with Margaret and their kids. He would show up early in the evening and celebrate with them. They thought he was leaving early Christmas morning to fly down to Florida to visit his old friend, Shelly. My father was Jewish, but he wasn't practicing in any way. Yet, he used his being Jewish as an excuse with both families to give him plausible reasons for distance on Christmas.

I remember leaving cookies out for Santa with my mom and my brother every Christmas Eve. Dad was never there for that. As a child, I accepted that, but now it's another one of those memories that are tinged with betrayal and hurt. He wasn't there with us because he was doing those kinds of things with his other kids.

Once I was older, and mom had moved to Arizona, our celebrations shifted. I would always arrive on the 23rd or 24th, but my father would never come until Christmas Day. He would say, "Oh, it's just easier to fly on Christmas. There's fewer people in the airports." We just accepted that too. Now we know it was a lie. He was always using the car store as an excuse, as well. My mother would often plead with him to stay for New Years, but he would not. He had to get back to the car store, he claimed. All those years he was in Arizona with us each Christmas, he had told Margaret he was visiting his college friend in Florida. Patty, my father's office manager, recounted a story to us from one time when she picked my father up from the house in Lake Forest to drive him to the office. She was chatting with my dad about the details of his double life being exposed, and he snickered about how Margaret believed he was visiting Sheldon in Florida all those years.

The rouse, of course, was not reserved for holidays. My father's evasiveness and his habitually scheduled absences were always a part of our lives. There was one weekend a month when he was supposedly off fishing with his friends. We now know that was also a lie. Sundays were also a day he carved out for Margaret and their family.

While he would occasionally spend a Saturday with them, typically he was with us. He would wake up Sunday morning and read the paper in bed with my mom, an activity my brother and I would interrupt to ask for the sports page or comics section. Then, around mid-morning, we would all have breakfast. Then, by around 11 AM, he would start saying things like, "Well, I better get ready. Got a lot of paperwork to do at the store." And by noon, he was with his other family.

That was his Sunday routine with us. Occasionally, my mother would put up a fight. I remember some heated arguments breaking out. "Why can't you spend a whole weekend with your family?" my mom would ask. She wanted him around more, but most of the time, she just accepted it the way it was. My brother and I usually had something going on during the day, and it wasn't seen as a big deal that he would be gone. Then by 10 PM, he was home again. Come to find out from Carolyn, this was their day to hang out with him and watch football together.

There are so many other things we now wonder about, many of which we are left to assume what was happening—such as the period in the 70s when my father suddenly started carrying a pager. He told my mother it was for work, but we now know this was the time when Margaret was pregnant with Carolyn. It's far more likely that the pager was a way for Margaret to reach my dad than it was that some legal case required him to carry it. Sadly, many details such as this don't add up or simply don't feel right in retrospect.

Another example was our unlisted phone number. Dad always insisted our number be unlisted, claiming he didn't want law clients to be able to find his number and address. However, my mother happened to look in a phone book one day and noticed a Norman Zimmerman listed in Glenview. She showed him and laughed it off as a silly coincidence. Of course, that listing was actually him—Margaret must've failed to ensure their number wasn't listed. It's wild to think about how many times he probably came close to getting caught.

The red flags continued well into my adulthood, right up to the point where the old man was finally exposed. In fact, in 2012, the year before his lies were laid bare, there had been numerous incidents and changes in his behavior that we brushed off at the time.

Since 2001, my mother had been living in Arizona. Despite the distance, my parents spoke every day and we still had numerous family gatherings and events every year. Then, in 2012, he just suddenly stopped participating in things. He was supposed to attend my mom's Aunt Dorothy's 100th birthday in March, in my mother's hometown. He did not attend with us. Then came Father's Day—a day I had chosen to visit in prior years. He tried to get out of it, which resulted in my brother deciding to stay home. In November, there was a family wedding Dad was supposed to attend, but he supposedly caught a cold and canceled. Finally, Christmas 2012, was the first time he had ever failed to make the holidays in Arizona. At the time, he was in the midst of selling the car store. He told us that the negotiations were stalling and requiring more time. Rather than cancel outright with us, he postponed day after day, peddling new excuses as to why the deal was not done and he could not yet leave. Of course, we now know that this sudden shift in my dad's behavior was likely because Carolyn's family, previously estranged, had started playing a larger role in his and Margaret's lives, which made his maneuvering much harder.

I wonder if he had any inclination or concern that the wheels were starting to fall off—that the demands of his two worlds were in so much conflict that eventually something would have to give. I imagine that some part of him felt that the hard part was over and he was in the clear once my mother moved to Arizona. Still, some part of him had to know that eventually, the truth would come out. Did he really believe he would get away with it?

My father had a way of giving each family just enough to placate us. While our family was his primary family and got to spend the most time with him, he somehow found a way to balance his time between us and them for decades. Each family had routines and excuses that he would use to justify those routines. Families get used to routines and everything seems normal. So, even though he was only spending 15-20 percent of his time with Margaret and their kids, to them, I am sure it felt quite normal. However, I am reminded of what my father told me during one of my visits while he was in rehab: "Mike, I don't think either woman was ever really happy with me."

That stands out. My father spent most of his life trying to balance these two lives, and by his own account, he failed to do so. He made two women and eventually two families unhappy because he couldn't do the difficult thing and own his mistakes.

As much as we've been able to piece together, lingering questions remain. We have no idea how he managed to pay for another house, let alone how he provided for a second family early in his career My father did well for himself, but an entire second household? A second set of children to feed and clothe? Insurance costs? Tuitions? It's just a lot of money, and it's out of the realm of what we thought would've been possible, given what we knew about his finances. Sadly, it's just another piece of the puzzle we will probably never find.

I still struggle with my memories. I probably always will to some extent. These pieces of my life and the feelings that accompany them are no longer simple recollections—they're now inextricably linked to my father's betrayal and deceit. Even simple, happy memories like fishing with dad have been tainted: I now can't help but conclude that this was just his way of providing an alibi for himself whenever he needed it. If he had never taken us fishing, his fishing trips would have seemed suspicious. It's hard to grapple with the fact that so many of my memories with the man I considered to be my best friend were not as I recall them. It's something that I think will always haunt me to some degree, even as I close that chapter in my life and move on.

There is only one aspect of my memories with my father that still feels very genuine—one area where the memories feel authentic. That was our shared loved for the Chicago Cubs. Unfortunately, following the exposure of his lies and the fallout with Margaret, that aspect of our relationship would also become damaged by his disloyalty and cowardice.

CHAPTER 14

ME, MY FATHER, AND THE CUBS

W hen you grow up in Chicago, you're either a Cubs fan or a White Sox fan. My old man was a Cubs fan, like his parents before him. As far back as I can remember, the Cubs were a part of my life. They were always on TV and dad was always talking about the team. He was old enough to remember the last time they had been in the World Series, back in 1945. Then he witnessed some great teams in the 60s when they had some real talent like Billy Williams, Fergie Jenkins, and Ernie Banks. With the family influence, it was only natural for me to become a fan, as well.

Wrigley Field didn't have lights installed until the late 80s. This was likely a disadvantage for the team, as it meant their players had to play all their games during hot summer days. But it worked out wonderfully for me as a kid. I would come home from school and the game would still be on WGN TV, the local broadcaster that brought every Cubs game to us. I became a bigger and bigger fan and got really invested in 1984 when they made it to the playoffs.

A genuine love for the Cubs was something that I came to share with my father. We would watch the games together during the season and speculate about their prospects during the off-season. It was an emotional connection we both shared with the team that we could share together. We shared in their highs and the many lows. My brother, on the other hand, was never a Cubs fan. I don't know if it was his way of defying my father or just being contrarian, but his team was the White Sox. My father hated the Sox. Whatever his reasons, the Cubs were a bond between me and my father—one of the only places where I didn't have to compete with anyone else.

It was the summer of '78 when my father took me to my first game. The Cubs were hosting the Pirates. We had seats right on the first baseline in right field. The whole experience was overwhelming but exciting. Wrigley is such a beautiful ballpark with a storied history. It feels like you're walking into a fabled place. The architecture has such character, and the park, being as old as it is, has a smaller feel than many of today's stadiums. There aren't really any bad seats in Wrigley. After watching so many games at home, it was pure joy to get to be there and experience it firsthand. It forever changed my experience watching games from home, too. Now I had context; I knew what it felt like in person. I could almost feel like I was there when watching it on TV.

The Cubs lost to the Pirates that day, which was not uncommon. Being a Cubs fan would never get you accused of being a front-runner. They had more bad days than good, especially when I was young when they were often referred to as *lovable losers*. But as a Chicago native, that didn't matter. The Cubs were a tradition, an inseparable part of the city's culture and history. And like many families in Chicago, they had become a tradition in our household.

Regardless of their spotty history, I was always an optimistic fan. I was just a kid and didn't understand the organizational flaws. Dad was always more realistic about their chances, but win or lose, it was something we shared. We went to many games.

While we did a few White Sox games for my brother, it was not common. Dad had a few friends from law school who went on to own the White Sox and even had season tickets given to him one year. He gave most of them away at the car store. We did get to see the Detroit Tiger's Jack Morris no-hit the White Sox in April of the '84 season. It was a miserable cold day, as can be the case in Chicago that time of year. I remember being underdressed for the weather and secretly loving the Sox being no-hit by the Tiger's ace starting pitcher.

Even as I got older, the connection my father and I had with the Cubs continued. Once my brother and I no longer lived in Chicago, we would fly back at least once a year, usually around my brother's birthday. And even though it was his birthday, we would usually all go to a Cubs game. Birthday or not, there was no way we were going to a Sox game! And eventually, as Dad got older, we started a Father's Day tradition where we would visit him and catch a game at Wrigley.

These were always really enjoyable outings for me and some of the fondest memories I have of my father. They're memories that are mostly untouched by his lies. This was something genuine we shared. He wasn't putting me on or creating an alibi he could later use to escape—It was just good fun. Wrigley has always been a special place for me, but now it holds even more nostalgia.

The last game I went to with my father was on Father's Day weekend in 2012. My brother and I had flown in and taken him to the game the previous year, and I wanted to do it again. He was getting older, his hip was giving him problems, and I wasn't sure how many more years he would be able to make it to a game.

But before my visit, my father started giving me signals that maybe it wasn't such a good idea for us to come visit that weekend.

He gave us a myriad of excuses about how he wasn't feeling that great and wasn't sure if he was up for it. Unbeknownst to us, he was trying to juggle his Father's Day weekend plans. My guess is that Carolyn and her kids were around, and it made it harder for him to break away for our yearly tradition.

My brother was resistant to the idea, as well. "Dad doesn't want to go, so I'm not going."

"I know, but I'm concerned about his health. I don't know how many opportunities we're going to have to do this with him. We should really go," I insisted. However, my brother's mind was made up and I ended up traveling alone.

My father and I went to the game and had a nice time. But I'll always remember after the game when we got back to the car. His cell phone was ringing. He told me he didn't recognize the number and ignored it. I'll never know for sure, but I would bet that it was Margaret calling, looking for him. He was probably supposed to be somewhere with them and had pulled one of his infamous disappearing acts. That was the last time my father and I saw the Cubs and the end of a Father's Day tradition that had gone back many years.

From my childhood days on through my adult years, my father was my best friend, and the Cubs were a fundamental part of the fabric of our relationship. We saw many memorable games together in person and on TV. In 1986, I was in a bad car accident, and after I recovered, we went to see the Cubs play the Astros. Legendary Hall of Famer Nolan Ryan was pitching for the Astros. The Cubs lost. In 2003, they were just five outs from the World Series and blew it, losing to the Marlins. That was the infamous Bartman game, where a fan reached over the wall and grabbed the ball.

We were well accustomed to the Cubs losing, as all Cubs fans are. My Dad often spoke of the '69 team that narrowly missed the playoffs. Letdowns were part of the fan experience. Nevertheless, we used to dream about what it would be like if they ever reached the World Series. We would talk about what it would be like and how much we would be willing to spend if it ever happened, knowing it would likely be expensive. If it ever happened, we agreed, it would be worth it to spend a considerable amount on such a historic experience.

In 2016, it finally happened. The Cubs made it to the World Series. Sadly, my father was not speaking to me at the time. After a lifetime of rooting for the Cubs together, the unthinkable had finally happened—our dreams had come true. But my father's lies had been exposed and the fallout from all of that had led to this. I wanted to experience it with him, talk to him about it, and share my excitement. But my best friend was no longer my best friend. The long-time dream of sharing in the Cubs World Series together was dashed.

I decided that I was going to attend, regardless. I flew home for the weekend of games 3, 4, and 5 and got tickets for game 4. Tickets were close to $4,000, but I had been waiting for this my whole life. Like so many Cubs games I had seen before, they lost that night. However, they won game 5 the following night to stay alive, then won game 6 in Cleveland, setting up the decisive game 7 at Wrigley. I had to be there and was able to score standing-room-only tickets for $1,600. I jumped on a plane that morning to Cleveland, checked into a hotel, and made my way down to the stadium area where I met my childhood friend, Andrew Lockwood. He and I had attended game 4 in Chicago, and he was heading to Cleveland anyway for game 7 since his brother lived in Cleveland. I ended up watching the game with Andrew, his brother, and his parents who had also come in from Chicago. There were a ton of Cubs fans at the game that night in Cleveland.

All said and done, the entire experience ran me about $7,000. It was money well spent. I have no regrets other than the fact that after waiting a lifetime for that moment, my father was not there to share it. I remember thinking of him, missing him, and grappling with all the hurt and other emotions that came with it. After everything that had happened, I felt discardable. Our relationship just didn't seem to be a priority and seeing the Cubs win the World Series without him really drove that home.

Two days later, I joined a million or so Cubs fans lining Michigan Avenue in Chicago and gathered in Grant Park for the victory parade and rally. It was the culmination of a lifetime of fandom for me and many others. As I watched the parade, my thoughts drifted back to my father. I wondered if he was watching at home—I was sure he'd watched the games. I wondered if he was thinking about me. Did he miss me?

It's easy to blame Margaret. After all, she and her family isolated him and made having a relationship with him impossible. The bitterness they held for us never made sense to me. I could see her having some sort of jealousy or resentment for my mother, the other woman in her eyes. But to hold a grudge against me or my brother felt petty and wicked. My mother always said, "I wouldn't have denied their kids access to their father. They're innocent victims." Still, as much as I hold Margaret responsible, it is ultimately my father's failure. He caused the situation through his lies and betrayal, and he allowed them to cut us out of his life. As I stood there watching the parade, I knew that the disappointment I felt was not just disappointment in him not being there; I was disappointed in him as a man and as a father.

Despite my better inclinations, I pulled out my cell phone and called him. The call, of course, went to voicemail. "Hey, Dad. I'm in Chicago, watching the parade. I was at games 4 and 7. I wish we were watching this together. I miss you. I love you."

I never heard back.

We should have been there together, celebrating. It would have been a once-in-a-lifetime memory, a capstone to the decades of wonderful memories we had together. Instead, I was left standing in Grant Park by myself, wondering why my father would ultimately choose to cut me out of his life. It was a moment I had waited so long for, and yet it now felt incomplete and diminished by his absence. The best memories I have of my dad—the only ones that feel genuine in light of recent revelations—ended in disappointment and sadness.

CHAPTER 15
MY FATHER'S CONFIDANT

What really keeps me up at night are the questions.

What was my father's true nature? What were his actual feelings about us? How did he manage to live a double life for so long? What other secrets did he have?

Those questions consumed my mind in my quietest moments. But others came to mind, as well. Questions about what he was like with this other family. Questions about my relationship with my father, what was genuine and authentic?

In many ways, the revelation of my dad's second life forced me into the role of an investigator. From the very beginning of this saga, there was information we needed and questions I wanted to be answered. The decent thing for my father to do would have been to provide me with those answers but despite multiple opportunities, he took those answers to his grave. I had gotten glimpses of the picture I was desperate to put together from talking to Carolyn but Margaret and my father had managed to burn my bridge to her before it could produce much. She was still in shock and disbelief when we spoke, and I have always wondered what else I could've learned if she hadn't been turned against me.

That brings me to Patty. Patty had worked for my father for 22 years, starting as an office manager and eventually becoming the treasurer of the corporation. During her time at the dealership, she became my father's most trusted employee, business confidant, and friend. Even after he sold the business in 2012, Patty stayed on to help him wind down the business affairs. There were decades worth of documents and files that needed to be sorted through and either shredded or stored. My father still had his apartment that he had gotten in the late 90s when my mother had asked him to move out after his affair with Molly was brought to light. This is where Patty and my father worked together to coordinate the remaining tasks.

From April 2013 through July 2014, Patty and my father worked out of his two-bedroom apartment, determining what had to go to the shredders and what had to be stored for seven years. Patty was also managing the remaining accounting responsibilities: outstanding obligations, worker's compensation audits, etc. There was a $600,000 pension liability that remained unsettled that my father eventually ended up having to pay, cutting deeply into his final sale proceeds.

In August of 2013, I reached out to Patty, hoping that she would be willing to provide me with information. While she didn't have any information about my dad's second family, she was surprisingly willing to help us learn more through her ongoing relationship with him. And that relationship was integral to my father at this point. Keep in mind, that my father was wheelchair-bound at this point, unable to get to and from his office or his apartment on his own, and Margaret was still totally unaware that he had owned the dealership at all—let alone his 36-year career there. So, my dad was entirely dependent on Patty to get where he had to be. She became his chauffeur; driving him to and from all his doctors' appointments, attorney meetings, bank trips, and pharmacy runs. She was almost always on call to handle his every need. While most of their time together was spent working from his apartment, she had lots of time to converse and pry for answers during their frequent drives.

Patty vividly recalls her conversations with my dad on the 30-40-minute drive from his home in Lake Forest to his apartment in Schaumberg. "Where does Margaret think we're going?" she asked him once. "To my law offices downtown," my father replied. The law offices that Margaret had no idea did not exist.

It was on one of these morning drives that my father disclosed to Patty that my mother was divorcing him. This gave Patty the opening to ask questions and my father revealed his secret. He told her about his double life and second family. Patty was stunned to hear all this— she knew my mother and my brother. She knew of my cousins, my father's nieces. For many years, she had thought she knew this man. She had seen his questionable behavior with Molly and had her suspicions but she would have never guessed his deceit ran that deep.

At first, my dad gave sparse details and shorter answers. But as Patty learned more, she noticed he seemed almost relieved to be talking about it, as if a weight were being lifted from his shoulder. He began to open up to her more and more, talking openly about the details of his 40-plus-year charade. His relief was palpable to her; he finally had someone he could talk to about it without fear of judgment or consequence. Considering that aside from being a father, my father's double life was probably the single most prodigious and time-consuming undertaking, it had to be beyond hard to never talk to anyone about it for four decades. Think about human nature and our desire to share our experiences with others. Just imagine having this giant secret that takes so much energy and constant devotion to pull off, and not being able to share it with anyone for fear that doing so would cause it all to come crumbling down. It must have been shameful. It must have been lonely.

"How did you pull it off?" Patty asked him.

"Money. A lot of money," he said plainly.

That's damn sure. Just providing our family with the standard of living he did was an achievement. To have enough to do it for an entire second family without anyone getting wise? That must've taken a hell of a lot of money. As such, the dealership was crucial to his pulling it off. It provided enough income to keep both households comfortably afloat and their finances completely separate. If at any point during his ruse, my mother had seriously pursued a divorce, it would have put him in an incredibly precarious situation. Any settlement could have disrupted his finances and the legal battle could have unearthed his second life.

Patty continued to ply my father for information, and I was able to gain insights about a lot of the questions I had.

There was no question that my father loved us. He bragged that my mother Ann was the smartest woman he knew. He boasted of her volunteer work and how she'd won Woman of the Year in Winnetka for her efforts to pass a funding referendum to renovate the local Police and Fire Department to build a woman's locker room for female officers and firefighters. It was clear from the way he spoke of her, that he had great respect for her despite his decades of cheating and lies. He also spoke with great pride about me, Patty said. He saw me as success-ful and independent and loved speaking to me about sports, politics, and world affairs. She told me that he was always excited when my brother and I would visit him for a weekend to attend a game. And while he undoubtedly loved my brother Alan, his comments reflected the distant and often tense relationship they had. I wish he had taken the time the know him more.

Tellingly, my father allegedly spent considerable energy lamenting how jealous he was of my brother and me. Life was easier for single guys these days, he'd say—it was harder in his day to get laid. That is perhaps, the single biggest flaw my father had: he was a philanderer and a womanizer. It is easy to see how that simple urge to get laid led him to bad decisions that trapped him in a life of lies. My father claimed he was born too soon and would have been happier coming of age in today's more relaxed hookup culture. He was probably right. Although, as I learned, that path leads anywhere but fulfillment.

Patty was also able to gain insights into my father's other family.

My father described Margaret as a stern woman with a quick temper who was always causing trouble. According to him, she had few friends and even her own mother didn't like her. She had assumed my father's last name, knowing full well all those years that she was not married to him—a fact she lied to her children and family about. My father somehow convinced her that he could not divorce my mother, however, she had no idea that he had a family with her and that was where he would spend all his time. My father would complain about all the issues Margaret had caused over the years, interacting with service workers in her home and in public. According to him, she had a history of run-ins and conflicts including with a window treatment company at her home and an incident with a TGI-Fridays employee that resulted in a police report. Based on my one experience with Margaret and what I had heard from her on voicemails my father had left me, this was not a surprise.

Margaret hated the fact that they never went on any family vacations together. That's a fascinating detail because it shows how discontent she was with the life she had chosen for herself. Of course, they never traveled; my father had no way to disappear from our family for that long.

Patty had also learned that their daughter Carolyn had been estranged from them for eight years following her marriage because neither of them approved of her husband. Carolyn's husband was a former Air Force pilot who was about 13-14 years older than her, and that was supposedly part of the issue my dad and Margaret had with him. Patty had a few interactions with Carolyn during the time she was working with my dad from his apartment, and those interactions went about as well as my last conversation with Carolyn. Carolyn was rude to her and once made a scene at the nursing home. She acted like "an entitled bitch," according to Patty. No surprise there, either.

My dad told Patty that their son, John, had endured challenges throughout his teenage years. He never attended college and worked at a grocery store as a night manager. My father described him as having social challenges which Margaret insisted on financially supporting. It seems that in both families, my father had a golden child and a child he was disappointed in—a child that might have greatly benefited from more support and guidance.

My father began unloading all sorts of details to Patty—finally having someone he could talk to, even brag about, his grand rouse. He told her how he used fishing as cover whenever he needed to hide, and how he had to keep a double set of the same clothes at each home so that neither family would ever catch him wearing something they didn't recognize. As such, he wore mostly blue suits, white dress shirts, and boring ties—never anything flashy or trendy.

It's still hard for me to imagine, lying to everyone you know; your parents, legal spouse, your children, friends, colleagues, and anyone with whom you ever came into contact over time, your every inter-action being twisted in an elaborate web of lies spun over decades. Having to cover your tracks so carefully for so long. It had to have been a massive burden. Of course, he had his accomplice—without Margaret's willingness to be a kept woman and lie to everyone she knew, he wouldn't have been able to pull it off. Ironic, given how little she actually knew and how unhappy she was.

As he told Patty, he easily fooled Margaret whenever he pleased with stories like where he would for Christmas every year. As far as she knew, he was traveling for work most of the time, and when Christmas came around, he would take off to Florida to supposedly visit his college buddy Sheldon Becker. Nope, he was in Arizona with us at my mother's, celebrating the holidays.

Once the divorce was settled and my father legally married Margaret, she and Carolyn began to act more entitled, and their behavior toward Patty became more hostile. Patty had kept a journal of her interactions with them to protect herself, as Margaret had threatened to sue her several times (God knows for what). Patty was not only exposed to Margaret and Carolyn's terrible treatment; she saw how awful they both were to my father. This cemented Patty's loyalty to me and our family. My father's apartment was filled with personal effects from our family: photos, gifts, and mementos. Patty made sure the photos my mother sent of our annual Christmas gatherings were left in the apartment for them to find, along with some risqué photos my father had of Molly.

Interestingly enough, my father had second thoughts after marrying Margaret. According to Patty, he spent several weeks musing about whether he could get the marriage annulled. Seeing how dra-matically her behavior shifted once they had gotten married was probably quite alarming for him. But at that point, he had made his bed and was stuck.

It was the summer of 2014 at that point, and the business activities were winding down. Margaret, now actually married to my father, demanded that Patty give her control of everything. She wanted the keys to the apartment and the storage facility where my dad's business records and personal effects were stored. According to Patty, they treated her with nothing but contempt. As far as they could tell, she had been involved in helping my father with his lifetime of lies. Neither of them seems very bright or capable of discerning the truth. They acted as if anyone associated with my father was their enemy and had to be purged from his life.

This resulted, on several occasions, in nasty and quite deplorable behavior from Carolyn and Margaret, aimed at both Patty and my father. On more than one occasion, when Patty was visiting my father at the nursing home in Lake Forest, Margaret and Carolyn would descend upon the scene, yelling and screaming, demanding she leave. On one such visit, the nurse approached Patty nervously to tell her that Margaret had instructed her to call and alert her to any of my dad's visitors. The nurse expressed discomfort and said she was shaken by Margaret's actions but was required to comply. She called and handed the phone to Patty, and Margaret proceeded to scream at her. "I will be taking Norman home and you will never be able to see him again!" On another visit, Carolyn called my father and he mentioned that Patty was visiting. Well, she went right to her mother, of course, who called up my father and berated him. Carolyn then called back a minute later to pick up where her mother had left off. According to Patty, my father couldn't get a word in edgewise as

Carolyn admonished him. "She is a clone of her mother," my father reportedly said, shaking off her behavior.

The sad irony of all this is that Patty was able to observe how little anyone visited him. My father told her that the only real visitor he had other than her was Margaret. Carolyn was infrequent and John had been by just once. It's wild to me that this family was so protective over who had access to my father and was content to let him rot in relative isolation in a nursing home just a few miles from their homes.

In early 2015, my father's health declined. Patty went to visit him again on February 25th and was denied access. Margaret had put in place a list of approved visitors: she, John, Carolyn, and Carolyn's husband were all that were listed. There was no risk to them letting her see him at that point; it was pure maliciousness.

Patty managed to be a friend to my father while maintaining her loyalty to my family. While I can never fully understand his actions, I am glad he had someone to talk to and be a friend to him during that time in his life.

I'm also personally indebted to Patty. Her time with my father and loyalty allowed me to glean insight into my father's actual life—not the charade he presented to us. Her cooperation and confidence provided me with more answers than my father ever did himself. Despite me having asked him, point blank, several times, he was never willing to confide in me. I still have questions—things that I wish I could talk to my father about. But he's gone now and all I have are what I can piece together. Thanks to Patty, I at least have some answers to the questions that would keep me up at night.

CHAPTER 16

ROCK BOTTOM

I t was another sleepless night in the summer of 2016. I tossed and turned and tried to get comfortable, hoping sleep would find me. My mind had other ideas, however. It raced with thoughts, recounting all I had learned, asking questions about what I still didn't know. I laid there for what must've been hours, memories of my dad surfacing and being reexamined. I would attempt to let go of these thoughts, knowing I needed to sleep, but my mind was so preoccupied. Anger, confusion, and disbelief came over me in alternating waves. In the morning, I would pull myself out of bed and head to work, my mind tired and weary. I was like that a lot in those days, although I didn't realize it at the time.

They say trauma impacts everyone differently and that when it's happening to you, it's easy to not notice the toll it is taking. For me this was true; I was so caught up in what was happening and in supporting my mother throughout it all, that I never stopped to think about how it could be impacting me. I was so distracted and absorbed in everything that was happening around me, that I didn't keep an eye on what was going on inside of me.

That was my experience for much of this ordeal. From the time I found out the truth in June 2013, and lasting at least a year and a half after that, I was just shell-shocked and lost in the weeds. In that state, you can't see the bigger picture. You can't even really gauge how you're feeling. You just exist, almost on autopilot, going to work, waiting for the next clue, revelation, or twist in the story. What was going to happen next? What other truths would I learn? In what other ways might Margaret or her family try to screw us over?

It was such a whirlwind of chaos and stress with no end in sight. Then, when it finally did die down, after my father had passed, it left me in a very confused, unsettled, and depressing place. I was spiritually, mentally, and emotionally exhausted. Sleep was sporadic—some nights it came easy because of how tired I was but others I would lie awake, just thinking about everything. My waking life was rote and without much emotional investment. I was constantly engrossed by whatever had just happened, whether it was something my father did, a development in one of the legal cases, or more of Margaret's drama.

What feels so particularly hard to overcome is that the person I adored and idolized my entire life was revealed to be such an awful person. I wrestle not only with the disappointment about the details we discovered but also with what it says about me. There's this sense of disbelief and regret; how could I mistake this person so badly? I tell myself that because I didn't observe any real overt abuse as a child, it was only natural that I would trust my parents.

I think about that trust now, as I spend the days with my son. These moments with him, watching him develop, are so precious and meaningful. I couldn't imagine being apart from him by choice like my father chose to be away from his offspring. I find myself asking, am I being overly sentimental about my son? Or was my father's behavior lacking any of the nurturing sensitivity a father should demonstrate for their children? His behavior seems sociopathic to me.

So I came to realize I was suffering extreme abandonment from the person I'd never expected. It was abrupt and jarring. And there were so many layers to it. Peeling them back was a never-ending experience over those first couple of years. Every time I discovered something and solved one mystery, it was like peeling off a layer of an onion, only the onion seemed to keep getting larger and larger the more I learned. Soon, the layers weren't just about my dad—they were about me. I was learning about myself.

Eventually, I ran out of pieces relating to my father. The legal avenues I had pursued had all closed at that point, leaving bitter feelings on both sides. Margaret had walled off my dad and I was left feeling isolated and hopeless, still wanting answers. And now, I had all these damn pieces of onion—pieces of myself and feelings about my father—strewn about. I was going to have to piece it all back together. But part of me was afraid to put those pieces together and see what they now added up to.

No matter how I tried to turn off my thoughts and bury my feelings by staying busy, going out with friends, or drinking, it all just consumed me, slowly pervading every aspect of my life. I tried my best to show up to work, handle my responsibilities, and maintain my relationships, because I wanted to present a façade to everyone around me. And despite how all-consuming my feelings and thoughts were, I felt I was doing a fairly good job keeping up appearances. And, I'm sure, if I'm honest, that I wasn't doing as great a job of it as I told myself at the time.

But I kept a lot of my relationships at arm's distance as a habit, and that meant I didn't really have anyone who knew me well enough and would've been comfortable calling me out or speaking up out of concern. I am sure that if my mother and I had been able to spend more time together, she would've seen a difference in my demeanor and behavior.

Those relationships I did hold closer than most turned out to be relatively ill-equipped to handle what I was going through. There was one circle of friends whom I had spent a lot of time with, sharing houses on the Jersey shore and socializing with year-round. Most of them completely turned their backs on me. They just couldn't be bothered to so much as hear about what I was going through. It was a drag on their party lifestyle, I guess. Some others saw it as an opportunity to take advantage of me, which surprised me. I had always been a very easy-going, non-competitive guy. I wasn't jealous of anyone or mad because of who got to date whom. And I always assumed everyone in that social group was equal. But it turned out that some of them had some jealous insecurities and harbored some negativity toward me, and that came out. I heard about it through mutual friends, and it was hurtful.

When I first found out about my father's secret family in 2013, the whole thing proved too much to handle for the woman I was dating at the time. She had just been through a pretty rough divorce and found it virtually impossible to separate what I was going through and my father's actions from those of her cheating ex-husband. Needless to say, that relationship didn't last. I proceeded to slide into several years of booze and bad girlfriends, many of whom could not show me the empathy I needed to help pull me from the depths of my depression. Again, I was too deep in simply surviving to recognize the bad choices I was making concerning whom I had surrounded myself with.

Lost in depression and grief, I sank further into the depths of isolation. I thought I was isolated after my relationship with my dad was lost, but the depression that ensued over those next few years led to even greater isolation. One which I didn't even realize I was submerged within. There was such a fog around me. I was lost. I wasn't close to identifying those facts. I drifted, ping-ponging through life without direction. Without positivity. Without awareness or sense of self. I drifted until I had the full realization that I needed to inspect those pieces of myself if I was ever going to heal. There wasn't one single event that led me to the realization I was at rock bottom. It was more from spending an extended period there before I started to see how foul and dark my existence had become.

Shock and then a general unsureness about how to handle it was a pretty common reaction when I would tell people about this. Once I had the wherewithal to realize just how depressed I was, I sought out a therapist, and the first woman I talked to had a similar reaction. I thought, well, this is great: even professionals don't know how to handle this level of bullshit.

CHAPTER 17
MY FATHER'S FACE

"**Y**ou've got your father's curly hair," was something I heard more than a few times as a boy. And I was proud to be my father's son. He was my hero, my role model, and my best friend. Unfortunately, it wasn't just his genetics my father passed on to me; I also developed a lot of his worst behaviors.

From early on, I absorbed the idea that a man should not allow himself to be tied down or obligated to a woman. My father didn't *ask* my mother to go fishing, he simply told her he was going. He didn't discuss his holiday plans with her, he *informed* her. While he never sat me down and told me, "Mike, your freedom and desires come before anyone else, especially a woman," the lesson was demonstrated nonetheless.

Pulling back the curtain on my father's double life and all his lies wasn't just an examination of his betrayal and how he had cheated all of us—it also forced me to eventually confront the truth of who I had become. The pain of the deceit and the lies were bad enough—reconciling that the man I had always trusted to have our best interest in mind viewed us as accessories to his life—but the real anguish came from realizing how his pathology and behavior had shaped the man I had become.

Through time and much introspection, I came to see that my father's negative influence loomed over both me and my brother. That was most evident in our relationships, particularly romantic relationships. Both Alan and I viewed them as fairly disposable and lacked any desire or ability to commit.

Dad used to always say things to me like, "Life's not a dress rehearsal." He was always reminding me that you only live once. In retrospect, I believe he may have been trying to impart some cautionary wisdom to me. However, I'd watched how he lived his life—how little he was home and how he would take off to whatever, whenever he wanted—and I took a different message from his warning. At the time, I took his advice to mean one thing: life is short so live it up. This was an unspoken mantra that fueled years of destructive behavior.

It's hard not to think that my father's lifestyle, the way he regarded women, and his attitude toward family life influenced my general disinterest and reluctance to have a family of my own. I viewed a committed relationship and a family as a burden. Why would I ever want that? It would limit my ability to do whatever I wanted when I wanted. Life was short, and I wanted to spend it living it up. I worked hard, like my father, and when I wasn't at work, I wanted to have fun. If my father's lies had not been exposed, I never would have seen the parallels, either. To me, my father *was* a family man and I was choosing a different path. It wasn't until I knew the truth that I could see the similarities in how we both chose selfishness over commitment and isolation over connection. That's what happens when you live by your own terms, owing nothing to anyone, and avoiding meaningful relationships; you end up isolated. My father must've felt incredibly isolated and lonely, which is why he was so eager to confess everything to Patty. And as I entered adulthood, completely unaware of the ways my father's influence was manifesting, I began making choices that I believed were making me free and happy but were leading to the same isolating place.

Look, I wasn't an angel. Far from it. My antics surpassed that of my father in the sense that I was part of a hookup culture that just didn't exist 50-60 years ago to the extent it does today. The norms and behaviors today are more casual and relaxed than when my father struck out on his journey of adult life. Nevertheless, as badly as I behaved at times, it paled in comparison to the lasting harm my father committed to two families.

There is a reckoning of sorts buried in this story. There is my history of reckless hedonistic pursuits, and the blinding haze around those activities which lifted only after the revelations about my father's behavior wreaked havoc on my life.

Ironic to say the least. Not until my life was unraveled did I recognize how terribly flawed my own life had become. It took all that for my wake-up call. And so much of my recovery was not just about gathering my awareness of what I had gone through for several years after the trauma that began in 2013, but also about coming to grips with the life I'd been living. I grew increasingly in tune with how eerily similar in some ways my adult life was mirroring that of my father's. I also recognized any chance at pulling myself out of the depths I found myself barely treading above water would require an honest assessment of where I wanted to go with my life.

I remember talking with my father, twenty years ago or so, about two women I was dating at the same time. He had very little to say about it, which makes sense now. But the one thing he did say was, "You know, you're not really being fair to either woman." I think back on that now and find that comment remarkable. It had to have been, at least on some level, a confession that he knew he was being unfair to both my mother and Margaret.

It's also clear, from that comment and his warnings about life not being a dress rehearsal, that my father didn't want me to make the same mistakes he had. It's a classic story of actions speaking louder than words. He told me and my brother the right words when he was around, but his behavior demonstrated other lessons that we absorbed subconsciously.

His words did nothing to prevent me from becoming someone who was lacking in responsibility, direction, or character. Those seeds were sewn deep through modeled behavior. It led me to decades of hedonistic behavior, chasing women, overdrinking, and being irresponsible with relationships. It was a toxic, self-destructive pattern I had no interest in breaking because until my father's lies were exposed, I never stopped to examine any of it.

Now, as a family man, I can say how isolating and unfulfilling the path I was on was. Words cannot describe how rewarding becoming a husband and a father has been. The love and peace my family gives me are like nothing else I have experienced in my life. It has given me meaning and purpose and filled my days with a joy that could never be reached through binge drinking and hookups. That is how I know that through all my father's cheating—his cheating on my mother and his cheating on us—he cheated himself the most. He deprived himself of the greatest joy there is on this planet.

I still have my father's curly hair. My face is shaped just like his as well. When I was a young adult, I would look in the mirror and see my father's face with pride. But for a while, after I learned the truth about who he really was, seeing his face looking back at me became a source of great pain and confusion. I still see his face when I look in the mirror sometimes, but I am slowly coming to a place of acceptance and gratitude. I'm grateful I learned the truth and was able to see how his influence was shaping my life so I could make those changes. Despite the pain it took to get here, I like who I have become, and I am beginning to accept that it was the truth and the pain that came with it that was the catalyst I needed.

CHAPTER 18
MY HEALING JOURNEY

There came a time, amid my darkness, when I was so buried in my misery that I could not even see the negativity surrounding me, or how it was affecting my choices at that time in my life. I was so lost and incapable of making any type of progress. It actually felt easier not to make choices. Some good people wanted to be a positive part of my life and help me, but it was easier to just keep doing what I had been doing. I continued to surround myself with booze and bad company. The choices I did make, the relationships I did invest in, were toxic—situations and people who only caused me more misery.

Eventually, I started to recognize the poor treatment and realize I needed to rid my life of negativity and focus on making positive choices. There was no question at the time it going to be difficult to extract myself from those circumstances. I was about to wage a battle on two fronts. One was with removing the negative influences from my life, the other was going to be with myself. I needed to be honest with myself about the changes I needed to make. Anything short of being honest with myself about a new direction would result in a relapse back into bad habits and bad relationships. I needed to surround myself with the right people, and I needed to immerse myself within the confines of a much more committed lifestyle than I had ever allowed myself to pursue. All at once, I was ridding myself of the wrong relationships, ridding myself of habits that were too eerily similar to my father's, and immersing myself in a different direction. All of that came on the heels of the most traumatic five years of my life. It was going to be a serious undertaking, however, one which ultimately led me to recovery and redemption.

Luckily, I was able to find a therapist who I connected with; an older gentleman closer to my father's age than my own. He had a lot of experience and wisdom, and he was really helpful by just allowing me to talk through and sort out all the crap that was in my head.

My recovery process was not quick. It took me years to fully reconcile with what had happened and to dig myself out of the hole I was in. For much of that journey, it was particularly hard because there was never any sense of closure; my dad was still alive and living with Margaret, and we didn't have many answers. It's hard to move on unless you can contextualize everything that has happened—to make sense of it and what it means to you as a person and your personal story—and you can't contextualize the experience without answers.

While I was sorting through all the shit in my head, I was also realizing who I wanted and needed in my life. I began to understand what had been holding me back when it came to personal relation-ships, and how I was avoiding commitment and real connection. Then I saw how much one person had truly come to mean to me.

I first met Beth in 2012, and I immediately concluded that she was much too nice for me. I was 41 at the time, and though she was nine years younger than me, she was light years ahead of me in maturity. I could tell she was looking for a stable and committed mate, and I was a severely untamed bachelor living a mostly wild and unserious life. I was a partier who followed my impulses, living a life of frivolity. She was serious about her career and spent her nights moonlighting as a fitness instructor. It was apparent to me very early on that she was an exceedingly good, reliable, and responsible person who happened to be an amazing cook and a lot of fun. She was a real catch, and I believed instantly that I did not deserve such a woman. She had her act so together that it bowled me over. I was used to dating people more like me—people who were stuck in a perpetual cycle of binge drinking, partying, and living life in excess. I was in a place where I was having too much fun running roughshod over the norms that applied to monogamous relationships and desperately trying to hang onto the last vestiges of my youth. To put it another way, I knew almost immediately that Beth was a keeper. I, on the other hand, was anything but.

So began our dance, more of a struggle or tug of war that lasted for years. We started slow, as I could not help but be drawn to her despite my inclination to run. I was not ready for anything serious but didn't want to let this one get away, either; I knew she was special. Then my entire world turned upside down in 2013 with the discovery of my father's scandalous lies.

Despite my shortcomings and hardships, Beth maintained a desire to be in my life. We got serious enough to know that we were quite a good fit. Despite my rather rowdy social life, I had always enjoyed healthy food and fitness, which definitely mattered to Beth. When I was able to step away from the chaos of the drinking scene and spend quality time in our relationship, it flourished. We embarked on trips together to places like Chicago, where I showed her my hometown of Winnetka. We drove around looking at the four different homes my parents owned during my life there, and she got to see the different schools I had attended. I showed her all around the village, seeing things like the house from *Home Alone*, and took her down to the beach at the lakefront, so she could see how different that waterfront Lake Michigan setting is from the New Jersey Atlantic oceanfront where she'd grown up. And, of course, we attended a Cubs game at Wrigley Field, and hung out for hours in surrounding Wrigleyville, soaking up the flavor that is a part of the local game day culture. We visited with my childhood friends who still lived in the area, and we dined at my favorite Chicago Pizzeria, Lou Malnati's.

We bonded over experiences like that Chicago trip, along with trips to Florida to visit her brother, Jason, and his family. Another trip to Montauk on Long Island for her other brother, Matt's wedding in May 2014. We always had so much fun together. Things were just so easy with her. We both shared an independent streak that complimented each other nicely, and we found a natural, great balance that felt like we were present for each other but never smothering. I knew if I ever wanted to settle down that she was the perfect person for me. We even discussed and discovered that we shared the same philosophy on parenting. She was perfect for me if I could ever get myself to the point where I felt worthy of her.

She was ready for a serious relationship that was moving towards marriage and parenthood. However, the combination of the family trauma I was enduring, along with my disrespect for serious matters like engagement and marriage left us at an impasse. I was vulnerable and could not resist the pull of the social scene. We went our separate ways, although we were never out of touch for very long. From there, I spiraled and was soon at rock bottom. I immersed myself deeper into the drinking scene, trying desperately to ignore the emotional pain surrounding me. Eventually, I looked around and took an honest account of where I was. I had brought so much additional drama and stress into my life through bad choices. Through much pain, I finally realized that I wanted more for myself than a life full of selfish people who could not care less if I was suffering.

With time, and through a lot of work, I got to a place where I was able to take a serious look at where I was in life and where I wanted to go from there. A big part of that was grappling with my father's influence over my life and recognizing patterns in my own life. I need to take a full accounting of what had happened, not just after I found out, but the entirety of this truth's implications on my entire life. Once you can survey what went wrong where and make sense of the damage, it gives you a direction to move toward healing. But it took time and distance from the trauma to be able to do that.

When my father died, it certainly didn't change what had happened. I still had to live with it and that it had happened. But I think that his being gone did mark the end of this dramatic saga and in that sense, the further I get from that point, the more context I have been able to gain. Because he is no longer with us, our ties to Margaret and her family have been severed, and in that sense, there is no longer anything aggravating the wound and preventing it from healing.

There is no single day you emerge from depression and think, "Ah, I'm cured! I've made it." Things just slowly start to get better and one day you notice the sun is shining again, and it feels good like it used to bask in its warm glow. One day the air is just a little fresher and your steps a little lighter. Your work becomes a little easier and you start to be more productive. That started to happen for me in 2018, and since then I have gone beyond simply recovery. I have used this experience and the lessons I was able to glean from it as motivation to be better and to live a more fulfilling, emotionally connected life.

Ultimately, that meant it was time for me to settle down a little and stop the party lifestyle. It also meant allowing myself to get serious with and commit to the woman I had been dating. I now recognized that for too long I had been following my father's example regarding my views and treatment of women. I haven't gotten two women pregnant at the same time and kept a secret family like him, but I had picked up on his emotionally detached and distant approach to relationships. Seeing his influence on that part of my life was a wake-up call. I realized I had been avoiding committed, long-term relationships, and I knew that I had lucked out and found a wonderful woman in Beth. I didn't want his influence to ruin that. I resolved to myself and to her to change, so I could have the life I wanted with her.

I knew I needed to make changes, and the reliability and structure of the life Beth lived were exactly what I needed as I recovered. I took my impulsiveness and desire to party and funneled it into a healthy outlet: my longtime love of skiing. Beth always supported my desire to head off chasing after storms on the west coast in search of fresh powder, and she reiterated her support of that going forward. Her only request was that once our child was old enough to ski, some of my powder-seeking adventures would become family trips. No argument from me. Once we had decided to seek a life together, Beth accompanied me to Jackson Hole, and despite not being a skier, she loved everything about the culture and aura of Teton Village and the town of Jackson. Our interests and goals were aligned, and the timing was right. Finally.

I think if my journey had ended there, I would still be a profoundly different person than I was before I found out about my father's secret. But this major change in my attitude and lifestyle also preceded the biggest, most important decision of my life. I knew there was a major concession I would need to make to stay with the woman I loved and, to my disbelief, I was ready and excited to do it: I was going to become a father.

CHAPTER 19

MY CHANCE TO DO IT RIGHT

The decision to become a father represented a dramatic shift for me. As I continued through the process of healing, it became clear to me that my father's influence was present in my romantic relationships. I saw too many eerily similar examples of careless behavior, as I was relatively avoidant when it came to commitment. I had spent too many years hedonistically carrying on without regard for the impact of my choices. That's at least part of the reason why my then-girlfriend Beth and I had been on-again/off-again for some time. When I realized how important she was to me, I decided I wanted to try and make it work on a serious, committed, long-term basis. Of course, I knew that she wanted to try and have a child together. She was 39 at the time and felt like her opportunity to do that was limited. So, if I wanted a life with her, I had to make two commitments—one to her, and one to our future child.

This was a downright frightening prospect for me. At 47, I had avoided any type of serious long-term, personal commitment for most of my life. I lived a bachelor's lifestyle of dating without expectations, partying every summer away, and going where I wanted when I wanted. The idea of giving all that up was terrifying. It wasn't just a matter of what I was giving up; there was a real fear that I wasn't cut out for it. But another part of me, the more rational part of me, knew it was exactly what I needed to do. I had been running from meaningful personal relationships my entire adult life. The lifestyle I had wasn't fit for a middle-aged man. As much as I had avoided it, deep down, I wanted my own family—though the thought of doing it was just terrifying.

I told Beth that I wanted to give it a shot. Neither of us knew if we'd have any luck because of our age, but we were fortunate enough to conceive fairly quickly. By the spring of 2019, Beth was pregnant and I had a 9-month countdown to get my life in order. We wanted to get married as soon as possible, and then we wanted to move into a bigger house. It's not that the townhome I had was insufficient; there were certainly people raising families in neighboring homes. We just wanted a little more space. Moreover, we wanted a fresh start for us. This was especially true for me, as I had many memories of my father tied to that old place. He was there when I closed on it at purchase and was there to help me move in. As part of this new chapter in my life, I had to consciously close the door on parts left unresolved.

This period flew by packed with milestones. We were scrambling to look at houses, go to doctor's appointments, get ultrasounds, and get married. It was a whirlwind of craziness, but it gave me something to throw myself into and kept me present instead of lost in my thoughts.

When the day finally came for my son to arrive, he proved a tad stubborn. Beth was in labor for 27 hours, from 2 PM Thursday until 5 PM Friday. I was completely exhausted by the end, and I had the easy part to play! I remember being there with her, through every moment, in awe of what she was doing. When our son finally emerged, the doctor let me guide him out and into the world, which was a really cool experience. It was the perfect start to my relationship with him, to be the first person to hold him and then transfer him to Beth. We were both so elated.

I remember being relieved that he was okay and healthy. That was our biggest fear leading up to that day, that there would be some sort of problem. But there he was, healthy and whole. We named him Weston. We were overjoyed.

It was, however, a tad bittersweet. I had this wonderful baby boy, and my mother had her first grandchild, but there was this feeling that it had all been delayed. If not for my father and his influence, it could have happened sooner. Additionally, there was this concern hanging over me like a shadow cast by his actions. I had thought of this man as my best friend and my role model for most of my life and he turned out to be far from worthy of that adoration. I think every new parent has doubts and concerns, but for me, there was an extra layer to it. I didn't want my son to grow up and realize I wasn't the man he thought I was.

Fortunately, what was rooted in fear also served as motivation. My son was an opportunity for me to be the man my father never was—to do fatherhood right. The universe was giving me another chance at a father-son relationship, and this time, I was in control. My whole experience was coming full circle. I could be the father my father never was. I could be my son's best friend without any hesitation or deception. I could be fully, genuinely committed to my new family. They would never have to wonder where I was or guess what priority they hold in my heart. When I held my son, I knew my life was never going to be the same. I would've loved him and tried my best to give him a great life, regardless of my experiences. But having been through all I had been through gave me additional impetus.

Weston infused my life with such love and wonder. It has truly changed me. Fatherhood has had such a huge part in healing me and putting me back together. I say without hesitation that my son saved my life. In a way, he gave me a place to put all that love my father had essentially rejected. Being with him during the first two years of his life has given me a new perspective on my own. It has been the joy of my life to watch him grow and develop—to see his personality starting to form. I am in awe of this little child. Each day has been one amazing milestone after another, and I have had the added benefit of working from home throughout. At any moment during the day, just seeing his smile, hearing his voice, and observing him running, or playing puts all of life's worries at ease.

I still think about my father a lot. Every meaningful moment with Weston, I am left wondering what my dad felt experiencing those things with me. I try to imagine it from his perspective, but it's hard. It's hard to imagine how he must've felt while maintaining his lies. Was he ever conflicted? Did it ever bother him to deceive everyone who cared about him?

As my son gets older, I expect to have more complex feelings about the memories of my father. It happens frequently now, and he isn't yet at an age where I have clear memories. The memories I have are accompanied by strange feelings. There are flashes of fond memories with pleasant emotions—evoked by something as simple as the recollection of his laughter—followed immediately by the pain of betrayal and rejection. These moments leave me confused and unsure about what I am supposed to do. Do I value those memories of the good times and cherish them despite my father's flaws, or am I supposed to purge myself of them? There is a sense of loss that I am left wrestling with, and I am still unsure what to do about it. I suspect time will help, and as time passes, I will create more memories with my son.

They say that healing from trauma requires you to recontextual-ize whatever negative experience you went through and incorporate it into a new story about yourself. You're essentially trying to take the experience your mind has rejected as being unacceptable because it doesn't fit into your personal narrative, and building a new narrative that incorporates what happened to you. It gives the trauma some sort of meaning in your life rather than just being a thing that happened. For me, my son did that. He enabled me to take what I had experi-enced and use it as motivation to be the best father I could be. His presence in my life allowed me to recontextualize my pain. It wasn't for nothing—it gave me the perspective and drive to make sure I did better than my father.

Fatherhood has made me vulnerable and compassionate in ways I didn't know were possible. I've become what I would call more humane and empathic. I've seen a side to myself that previously didn't exist. That personal growth resulting from becoming a father is so rewarding. And yet I can't revel in it without dwelling on the lingering feelings about my dad. Question if he felt the same emotions I do about being a father. After all, his experience with fatherhood was dramatically different than mine. He became a father to a son with a mistress, only to become a father again to me with my mother just 14 months later. Talk about having conflicting feelings. I'm so happy I don't have that conflict with my devotion to my son. Still, as I progress on my journey as a father I can't help but keep wondering about my dad's experience and then doubt that I was receiving what a young child deserves from his father. I couldn't imagine depriving Weston of my undivided love and attention.

Weston will never have to wonder if his memories with me are genuine. He'll never have to ponder as an adult if there were other places I would have rather been. He'll never have to stop and examine our relationship to determine which parts were authentic and which were lies.

I don't think those complex, haunting memories of my father will stop. I suspect I will have those for the rest of my life, but it feels different now. There is meaning I can draw from the experience, and I have my son and my love for him to fill that hole. He has been such a blessing to us, and it has renewed my passion for life. I want to show him so much and be around to share in his experiences.

My only hope is that when he looks back on his childhood and his memories with me, he can say that I played a positive role in his life. That he always knew I was there for him. I hope he will never have any doubts about how much he meant to me, and that every memory he has of me will feel genuine and authentic. I think it's natural for fathers to want to give their children so much. But for me, the most important thing I can give him is my undivided love, my honesty, and my devotion. Those things my father was unable to give me. And yet, I badly miss my dad. I miss the conversations. I miss his voice on the other end of the phone. I miss speaking with him. I miss the dad I knew before the curtain was pulled back on his duplicitous life. But I had to shut the door on those emotions and with that departure, I also had to depart the life I knew. I cannot reconcile still adoring who my father was before June of 2013. I cannot compartmentalize him into two people, separated by my knowledge of who I thought he was before June of 2013 versus what happened after that moment. My evolution contains two facets. The wall I've had to put up around who my father was and what the learning experience meant for my life. I never want Weston to have to reconcile his feelings about me the way I was forced to do with my father.

EPILOGUE

Ever since discovering my father's double life, and gathering information about who the other family was, there was always a mysteriousness around my half-brother, John. We were able to uncover minor details like his date of birth, however, unlike his sister, John did not have much of a digital footprint from which we could learn anything. Carolyn was on Facebook, and for a while, after we spoke, she and I were connected on that platform. John, on the other hand, was a relative ghost. The little we knew about him was from the details my father had told us when I'd asked about him in 2013 and 2014. My mom got some details from my dad, as did my dad's business manager, Patty. The only details I was able to glean from Carolyn about John were during my initial conversation with her. As she was digesting the details she had learned from me and my mother that day, she remarked, "My brother is going to have a hard time with this." Well, Carolyn, we were all having a hard time grasping these details of Norman Zimmerman's double life.

Still, we knew very little about John other than he was supposedly a night manager at a grocery store, and according to my dad, he was not college material and had not really accomplished much. That's fine. Everyone's version of success is different, and I certainly understand if John's childhood had been less than perfect since I was aware of the circumstances my father had exacted upon all of us. Yet, I still felt like John probably held a lot of clues to unanswered questions about our father, and as I consider things from my perspective, I cannot imagine he didn't have questions too. Perhaps ignorance is bliss, or perhaps John and Carolyn had been so lied to that they bought into the idea that our family and my father's legal marriage to my mother for over four decades was not real.

Whatever the case, I always remained shocked at the lack of curiosity exhibited by John and Carolyn. Ever since Carolyn had repeatedly acted like her mother's enforcer, trying to force a wedge between my father and any of my family or his friends, I had long since moved on from trying to have a relationship of any kind with her. John, I thought, was perhaps someone I could have a conversation with at some point. He and I had not exchanged any overt bitterness toward one another. Perhaps, if I connected with him, we could provide each other with some answers and closure.

However, finding him was another story. Over the years, various internet searches had never turned up any valuable information. I had his address from the law firm that handled my father's estate, as all four of my father's heirs and our addresses were listed on the documents we received after my father's passing. In early 2022, I tried sending a letter to him at that address, however, it was returned and denoted as an incorrect address.

A few months passed, and as I was doing some research, I came across a website that appeared to have more information on John than I had previously been able to discover. The same physical address I had attempted to send my letter to was still appearing, causing me to question if my letter had actually arrived at the correct address, but John had refused it. But the potential goldmine was a link to an affiliation connecting John to the Lake Geneva Fishing Club in Wisconsin. I found that to be an interesting connection, as Lake

Geneva was where my grandparents had owned a boat when I was a young child, and I still have early childhood memories of being on their boat with my parents. John never knew our father's parents; however, it makes sense that my dad likely took John fishing at Lake Geneva over the years. Lake Geneva was a place my father enjoyed going to and harbored warm memories of his father. I clicked on the link to Lake Geneva Fishing Club, and it pulled up a membership roster from 2018. Sure enough, there was John along with his email address, cell phone number, and physical address (the same address where I'd sent my letter). Perhaps I could finally make a connection and speak with John!

Before calling his cell phone number, I thought about potential outcomes. I kept landing on he won't recognize my number and will let it go to voicemail. I hit send and waited as the phone rang a couple of times, and then to my surprise, someone answered. There was just silence on the other end, so I said, "Hello. I am trying to reach John." He replied in a deep monotone voice, "Speaking." I could not believe that after almost 9 years into this ordeal, the mystery of finding John had finally been resolved. "This is Mike Zimmerman, your half-brother," I replied. Unfortunately, it quickly became apparent that John was somewhere on the spectrum of either living in utter denial, unwilling to accept the truth, or having been brainwashed by Margaret and my dad. After a half second or so of silence, he chuckled and said, "I do not have a half-brother." Click. Silence. He'd hung up.

I tried to put myself in his shoes and determine how I would have replied if the tables were turned. At the very least, I probably would have said, "What do you want?" Or perhaps his reply was his attempt at defiantly trying to stick it to me, as if to suggest I really do not exist in his universe and that his family unit was the only family unit. Whatever the case, I know he sat in the courtroom along with his sister and his mother the day my parents were divorced, and he listened to the proceedings that day which cemented the truth about my parent's legal marriage, as well as the truth that his mother and father had lied to him and his sister their entire lives.

At that moment, I was surprised he did not want to know anything at all. It had been two years since our father had passed, so if there was ever a time at which the emotions of the entire situation may have settled down, this was it. I immediately tried calling him back after he'd hung up. I got voicemail, which was a good thing. I proceeded to leave him a voicemail letting him know he is correct that he does not have a half-brother, but rather he has *two* half-brothers in Alan and me. I went on for a couple of minutes, detailing for him that our father's double life was real, and despite what stories he may have been told, all of this did happen. We were living in Winnetka since 1973, while they were stashed away in Glenview, just 6.3 miles from the homes we lived in during the 1970s, and eventually 6.8 miles in the homes we lived in during the 80s and 90s. I detailed to him not only information from our lives but also details from the last nine years—details that only someone with insider knowledge could have known. I let him know the purpose of my call was to help clear up any questions or misconceptions that exist about us and him. I did not bring up his mother at all, as I was trying to keep the focus on the relationship between us as half-brothers. I also made sure to mention something that I've yet to see openly communicated by him or Carolyn, and that was all of Norman's children—all four of us—were victims. We were all victims of the choices our father made. We had different upbringings, and while we spent more time with our father than they did, we were all negatively impacted by our father's choices. Whether or not John listened to the voicemail is something I will probably never know, but I at least spoke my truth and tried to extend that branch.

I feel for John because based on the details I've learned, along with what my father shared with us, John likely had the hardest road of the four of us children. His early formative years overlapped the birth of my brother and me, the death of his first sister, and the years in which my father was spending a lot of time taking over my grandfather's business and then eventually, dealing with my grandfather's death. Those things all occurred by the time John was six years old. Then his second sister, Carolyn, was born, and she likely took her share of the spotlight away from John. I totally get it if John harbors resentment about the situation. However, any resentment toward my family is misplaced. The only thing John experienced over the last nine years with me, and it was second-hand, was me fighting for access to my father. Knowing how much my father meant to me, I could never imagine trying to deny any child access to his or her parent.

AFTERWORD

Dear Weston,

If you are old enough to read this letter someday, then I know you will understand the meaning of these words. I also anticipate our lives together have been filled with fantastic memories and father-son experiences. What I want you to know is that beyond the memories of our experiences together, there is a much greater meaning to the role you have played in my life.

As you grow older you will learn about my life and your grandfather Zimmerman. You will also learn that you came into my life at a time when I badly needed you to arrive. You changed your mother's and my life so much when you arrived, and I was absolutely thrilled to be a father to a son. Something I did not realize before your arrival was just how positive an impact you were going to have on my life. I knew responsibilities would shift, and our time and energy would be focused on raising you. We showered you with multiple affectionate nicknames like Munchkin, Munch, Little Munch, Little Buddy, Bubby (which evolved from a mix of baby and buddy), and our favorite, Baby Weston. However, I quickly realized there was another name that applied to you.....my hero. All 7lbs, 1oz of you! I became mesmerized by you every moment of each day. I think that is a common feeling first-time parents feel for their newborn child, and we were in love with you from the moment we first held you.

When you arrived, I had exited a difficult time in my life that had stretched for several years. Your arrival was the milestone in my life that shifted my trajectory, giving me a newfound purpose. You were the new chapter of my life that badly needed to start, and I cannot thank you enough for making that happen. I came to realize how much your arrival and influence saved me. Each day, week, and month with you brings exciting new milestones and experiences which draw me closer to, and deeper into my history. A history that until I realized the joys of being your father were previously hazy and unclear. My own father's failings led me to discover myself, and through that journey, I discovered why I needed to become a father. I can see my life clearly now, both past and present, in ways I never imagined. I am aware more than ever that you, Weston, have been the glue that pieced my life back together. I say that not to burden you with pressure or unrealistic expectations. Rather, I say it because your mere presence alone saved me.

What made you my hero is how my life changed as a result, and how much meaning you have given my life. The journey from your first days as a tiny helpless baby through today as a wildly energetic, funny, and talkative toddler has been nothing short of a dream come true. Each moment witnessing your "firsts" has kept your mother and me in awe of you. First smiles, sounds, giggles, crawls, steps, words, and even naughty moments have provided us with sheer joy. We often find ourselves looking at each other marveling over something new that you just did, leaving us laughing and wondering how or where you learned that new something. There is an excitement to waking up each day, anticipating seeing you, and then gathering you from your crib. Observing the excitement on your face, and witnessing your enthusiastic joy as you play, is equally as exhilarating for us.

Finally, nothing is more meaningful than hearing your voice cascading throughout the house, especially when I hear the words, "See

Daddy" as you express your desire to see me, or when I walk in the room and I hear, "Hug Daddy." Even when you misbehave and launch toys, pillows, and just about anything you can get your hands on across the room, it is hard to stay mad at you for very long. You flash that smile at us and laugh away as we scramble to gather up whatever it is you just tossed across the room. And then as you sense our dismay, you inevitably reach for us and express your desire "try again."

It is impossible to say no to you as we adore you so much. My world is so much better with you in it, and you have shined so much light on what was a dark time leading up to your arrival. As you grow, I grow. You are responsible for my life growing in the right direction, and I am forever indebted to you for that. But this isn't just about me.

So much of what you have done for me has given me a window into what my role is as your father, ensuring that you in turn grow up with the character and ability to someday be a terrific father too. Where my father failed me, you have opened the door for me to see what I was missing and ensure you do not go wanting. You will have the role model I did not have, and I can assure you as a result you will lead a richer more fulfilling life. So much of what I want to impart to you will be through our shared experiences, and the examples you witness in our daily life.

Make no mistake, you are the best thing that ever happened to us, and I want you to have the world. Accomplish whatever you set your mind to and pursue the life that makes you happiest. Just promise me one thing: what you take away from our life together gets shared and repeated with your children someday.

ACKNOWLEDGMENTS

As I approached writing these acknowledgments, I thought back on the entire journey. I thought about the people in my life when this situation fell into my lap. Where I was in mid-2013 was a drastically different place than I am now in late 2022. This experience was so unique, and I quickly learned I was traveling unchartered territory not only for myself but also for the others with whom I shared my troubles. There was nothing easy about this experience, and often it was the real genuine friends who made all the difference when I was struggling. As such, there are many people to thank.

First, I owe a ton of thanks to my wonderful mother. She endured hell alongside my brother and me as we unwound the details of my father's secret double life. Her perspective is quite different than mine, as she looked back in her golden years at the prior 50 years of her life in which she knew my father, and knew she had to make the best of what little time she might have left. She successfully encouraged me to overcome the challenges this situation threw at me and look forward to living as full a life as I could without allowing this to be a permanent drag on my life. She was there for me throughout, growing us closer as a result, and she has been the best mother a son could ever hope to have.

My brother Alan. You and I took a different approach to how we dealt with our trauma, however, our conversations about our father and what we discovered about him were an important part of the recovery. You never connected with our father the way I did. Perhaps it is easier for you to let go of it all knowing you were not as close to him. I hope you are at peace with this situation, living life positively, and growing from the experience we endured.

I want to thank my publisher and editorial team at Conversation Publishing, Keith Farrell and Eland Mann. You guys were with me throughout the entire creative process, and it has been a pleasure working with both of you. Your ideas, your expertise, and friendly approach to the process were essential, and I truly appreciate your guidance and support. Special thanks to Denise Painter for your help in finding Keith and Eland to launch my project.

Special thanks to my attorney Daliah Saper and her staff at Saper Law Offices in Chicago. I cannot thank you enough for your advice and support. It is truly an honor and a privilege to work with you. Your clients are very fortunate to have you!

Then I think about the many friends I leaned on, some of whom never knew this story, but have been there for me with their friendship. When I was at my lowest and extremely lost, you supported me with your presence and your kindness at a time when I badly needed kindness in my life. I cannot express enough how alone I felt throughout this ordeal. For the friends who knew about my story and stuck by me, never judging me or my trauma, I cannot thank you enough. I rarely let on how horrible my life felt during the years between 2013-2018. Perhaps you observed it, knowing I wasn't myself. Whatever the case, you should know how much I valued your presence in my life. Whether it was grabbing a beer, watching a football game, attending ball games, or hitting the ski slopes, I needed the support and distraction from the personal trauma I was battling. Please know I do not take your friendship for granted, and I value it as much today as I did when I was at the lowest depths of my depression. Thanks to so many of you, with special mention to the following individuals, starting with my childhood friends, some of whom go back to first grade and who knew my father: Andrew Keith, John Sexton, Mike Heinz, Andrew Lockwood, and Ben Bass. Thank you. Lockwood, that magical week in October 2016 when we attended two Cubs games in the World Series, watched the other games in the bars of Wrigleyville, and attended the victory parade in Grant Park will always be a cherished memory. Being at game 7 in Cleveland with you, your brother and your parents was truly special. Continuing thanks to the friendships more local to my current home, some of which date back several decades (utilizing nicknames where appropriate): Scot Carriker, Matt Ryan, Fordie, Mike Lihota, Missy Weisberg, Leigh and Dave, Beach, Fish, Katie, Jack London, Bear, Orca, Mike Missig, and Matt and Meghan Kelly. Thank you. You all played a role in supporting me whether you knew it or not. Our busy lives bring us in and out of face time with one another, however, you have all contributed to my recovery simply by being a friend.

Many of my mother's friends from Winnetka were very supportive and helpful, in particular her close friend, Maureen, who went above and beyond in the early days of the ordeal.

Longtime friends of my father, Howard Bass and Harvey Wittenberg. Thank you both for your time in accompanying me to visit my father.

Thank you to my former therapist, David, who had the calming insight to bring much-needed perspective and clarity to my mindset as I wrapped my brain around the entire experience. Many of our conversations were challenging, however, much needed.

Patty, my father's long-time office manager. It has been a pleasure knowing you over the course of approximately 30 years. You were a loyal employee of my father and you were always kind to my family. I greatly appreciate your efforts to help me since 2013 as I desperately needed your support in staying connected and in touch with my father. Being my father's confidant at work for all those years enabled the dialogue he had with you in 2013-14 where he divulged many previously hidden details about his double life. The information you provided me about the situation as you witnessed it was crucial. Huge thank you!

Last but not least, Beth and Weston. Thank you both for being the glue in my life that not only put my life back together but also instilled a purpose and direction I badly needed. There is no way I would have landed on such a positive trajectory were it not for the two of you. Beth, you have been a champ in supporting this endeavor as I spent countless hours writing, revising, and asking for your input on this effort. You never doubted me, and always provided me with the support that kept me inspired to see this project through to the finish line. Weston, when you are old enough to read this, you need to know what an inspiration you have been to me. As the years with you speed by, it puts more distance between me and my dad, and I feel the importance of being your dad growing more and more each day.

ABOUT THE AUTHOR

Michael S. Zimmerman was born in Chicago and raised in Winnetka, IL. He graduated the University of Rochester and lived the post-grad ski bum life working at Arapahoe Basin, Breckenridge, and Keystone ski resorts in Summit County, Colorado, Michael has spent the last twenty-seven years working in the mutual fund industry. He has also pursued entrepreneurial interests in real estate and classic cars, both of which were influenced by his father's business pursuits. In Michael's free time, his never-ending pursuit of chasing powder on the ski slopes of Utah, Wyoming, and Montana is front and center, only to be superseded by his love of spending time with his family. Michael and his family reside on the east coast.

For more from Mike, check out michaelszimmerman.com.

CPSIA information can be obtained
at www.ICGtesting.com
Printed in the USA
BVHW080531010223
657527BV00013B/485/J